The Insider's Guide to Autism and Asperg

Also available as an e-Book, published by Kognosimages/Vook of New York City and downloadable on all major formats, including Amazon, i-Books, Google, Kobo, Barnes and Noble.

© 2013 Ian Charles Ewart Hale.

ALL RIGHTS RESERVED. This book contains material protected under International and Federal Copyright Laws and Treaties. Any unauthorized reprint or use of this material is strictly prohibited. No part or parts of this book may be reproduced or transmitted in any form or by any means, electronic or mechanical, including photocopying, recording, filming, or by any information storage and/or retrieval system without express written permission from the Author/Publisher

Contents:

Book Reviews

The Insider's Guide to Autism and Asperger's

Preface-about the author

Introduction

Chapter one- The history of Autism and Asperger's Syndrome

Chapter two- What Autism is

Chapter three- What Asperger's is

Chapter four-The Significance of Autism and Asperger's Syndrome

Chapter five-The Roots and Theories of Autism

Chapter six-Autism and Genetics

Chapter seven-OCD and a cat called Smike

Chapter eight-PTSD and Autism

Chapter nine-The Left-handed connection

Chapter ten-Boys and Girls

Chapter eleven-Early Diagnosis

Chapter twelve- Two Views on Asperger's

Chapter Thirteen- The Whole Body Condition

Chapter Fourteen- Help is at hand

Conclusion:

Selected reading and Resources:

Credits:

Disclaimer:

Reviews of this book:

1. "Dr. Hale has achieved with great success an in-depth knowledge of the leading viewpoints on a personal level and clinical evaluation into the definitions, findings and meanings through professional research as a top Autism Specialist in this increasingly important subject. He takes the reader into the vast and complex world of Autism in an easy to understand profile of the knowledge and research in these areas and the profound impact they have on people learning to cope with them in their daily lives. In Society today where the population Ratio has been going up for Autism in various Countries Worldwide and primarily in America, especially the States of California, Texas and Arizona it is vital to have a reference Manual easily available to help those affected by Autism, in all its

forms and stages. This book is that Manual and invites the reader to come past the door to reveal what it is like to live inside the Autistic world to better educate Society as a whole. Overall the Book is descriptive, well-written, staggering, profound, suburb and outstanding. It merits the highest the praise.   A 10+ "must read".

The National League American Pen Women-Nashville Branch:

2. "Given the increasing numbers of children being diagnosed with autism, parents should welcome this book as a very valuable resource. Dr. Hale is himself a person with Asperger's who has dedicated most of his adult life to research and advocacy. His Guide is easy to read and understand, full of insights. He writes from a unique, personal perspective, with warmth and understanding: Highly recommended".

CIS Review of Books July 10th, 2013.

"A super read: crammed with anecdotes, history, anger, practical tips, science, theory and medicine from someone who's there. Like no other book written on Autism, it takes no prisoners, unsentimental, heartfelt and at times controversial in challenging accepted positions and practice without losing its targets or sense of compassion".

Michael Wilkinson, Glasgow Scotland.

Dr. Hale Podcasting on Autism

Preface-A note about the author:

To be clear and come clean....It is important to put this book in its proper context by knowing a little of its origins. Autism is an indivisible part of me; it informs goads and limits.

Technically; I am Asperger's Syndrome, with mild Dyslexia, moderate Dyscalculia and Attention Deficit Disorder. To the best of my knowledge these traits have passed through previous generations of the family through the paternal side for more than two hundred and fifty years back to the behavioral records and family archive of a forebear who was in the notorious Bethlehem Hospital in London .The original "Bedlam", a mental Asylum in the mid eighteenth century, where the public were charged an admission fee by the warders to spectate on and bait the sufferings of the inmates as a form of "public entertainment "and private money-making greed (Hale Family Archive: Gloucester County Records Office).

There are times when we should ask ourselves how far we have truthfully come in the field of mental and indeed physical health since then. The despicable child and adult abuse case of the English popular "entertainer," Jimmy Saville; being a prime example, with many of his crimes being committed in public hospitals against patients, some Autistic.

Currently there are two male and two female cousins with various Autistic statements- overall about forty percent of my generation. In the next generation, the eldest child of one of those is identified as Asperger's, and has exceptional talents in the fields of art, sport, and Natural Sciences, another is Dyslexic. There may be more, who knows? To paraphrase a joke-"Autism doesn't run through the family, it ambles gently around getting to know everyone personally" ☺.

As for me, I was blessed beyond words by the effort, support and encouragement I received from my amazing parents and

Grandfather Ewart who always backed and believed in their "strange little boy" who grew into a writer, researcher, cat lover, Autism advocate, teacher and Consultant. My Father was a Royal Air Force pilot and my Mother a Royal Navy Nursing officer. I am from the historic City and County of Bristol, England, a member of British Mensa, the Accademia Costantiniana and a graduate of Portsmouth, Bristol and Bath Spa Universities. My professional background is in Further and Higher education, Special Education Needs, SEN organization and genetics.

Being a writer and practitioner specializing in Autism is one thing, but I hope that by actually being one to bring a new dimension to its understanding and implications, which is the principle reason for writing this book-only someone who lives it truly knows what it's like- this isn't academic theory or clinical observation- this is how it is and how it lives, good and bad. There is a point to this reverie-because of this family experience, autism is a part of normal life for me and this understanding lends a unique, powerful and sharply different perspective to both assessing and then providing a high quality of educational and life experience for affected people, whether children or adults-as each has their own particular viewpoint and needs. Autism is for life, including senior care. A fact seldom considered by social agencies-No-one "grows out" of Autism, it's not "a phase".

Introduction- Opening the Door:

Welcome: there have been many excellent and informative books and movies about autism, Tony Attwood, Wendy Lawson and Vera Quinn are three of many such authors, there are also thought-provoking movies like "Rain Man"(1988), "Mercury Rising"(1998) and "My name is Khan"(2010).

Additionally there are some fine websites such as www.Oasis.org and www.autismlink.com/ together with the websites of the famous Tomati and Karolinska Institutes in Stockholm, Sweden, the London UK publishers Jessica Kingsley and the superb www.dyslexia.org which deal minutely and accurately with a broad variety of the issues in this increasingly high-profile subject.

However most of these examine only one or two aspects of "The Autism Spectrum", as it is known, at a time and of which

Asperger's Syndrome is but one piece. Furthermore, they tend to fall into only one of three distinct categories: namely Self Help, brilliant but impenetrably worded academic publications, which concentrate on scientific research and theory and finally, very long books of pure description, helpful to teachers and doctors for diagnostic purposes and education strategies, but lacking any real background information or warmth which would place the subject firmly in its context and enrich the everyday lives of those affected by these conditions. This book is intended to fill in some of the gaps between these categories and humanize the subject, as well as to shed some fresh insights upon it.

It avoids jargon and so-called "New Age Psychobabble" and seeks to demystify and rectify the problems inherent in Autism by examining in clear terms the whole panorama of the subject, not just individual bits; beginning with its history and including practical advice at every level, yet without being an overblown medical-type textbook. It will unravel medical, psychiatric and psychological terminology to reveal what autism actually is and what it means to be autistic in day-to day life and then analyze its strengths and weaknesses to offer practical and constructive advice on dealing with it directly on its own terms, as it affects each individual.

It is a comprehensive look at the subject, drawn from a number of avenues of thought and knowledge, including anecdotal ones, as well as a series of ideas, research and commentary gained from numerous sources and from around the world. It cannot though claim to be definitive by any means, it is a guide. A complete, science-based understanding of the subject is still a long way off and any book or person, who claims to have all the answers, doesn't!

It is vitally important to acknowledge-as few doctors or teachers are willing to do-that autistics ("autistics" is a bit of a tricky, old-fashioned word, so from now on, we shall largely use the modern one "Autists") are people first and patients who happen to have a form or forms of autism, second. While accepting that resources were already limited before the economic crises of today, what is unacceptable is that the existing funding is being cut once again - and solely because autistics are a minority voter group-only around 2% of any given population- a cowardly form of social targeting and victimization.

A further aim of this guide is to inform and by so-doing empower all those whose lives are touched by autism to speak out against the discrimination and harassment that Autistics routinely suffer at the hands of largely uncaring or uninformed societies and institutions across the world on a daily basis.

Chapter 1

A Brief History of Autism and Asperger's Syndrome:

Throughout history there have been accounts of certain behaviors, mannerisms and personal characteristics which we now recognize as being unique to autism by both contemporaries and biographers of some famous-and not-so-famous people. A few of these are Microsoft founder, Bill Gates, artist Vincent Van Gogh, film-makers, Steven Spielberg and Tim Burton, Michelangelo and the great physicists Albert Einstein and Nikola Tesla all of whom-and others- we shall look at again more closely from time to time.

Albert Einstein, physicist
ca. 1919

The word "Autism" itself has its root in the ancient Greek "autos" meaning of or in "The self". This is the first, vital clue to the understanding of an autistic person. Their situation is such that they are forced by nature to "live in their heads" to a far greater degree than non-autistics. It is not a choice; it is a form of isolation and self-containedness, of being imprisoned or "closed in", within oneself. It is no coincidence that the word "automaton"- a robot, comes from the same linguistic source.

There is a very unresponsive, expressionless quality about all Autists which is noticeable, as is an absence of physical feedback (Non Verbal Communication-abbreviated by psychologists as NVC-a.k.a "Body Language") particularly in finding the correct interpretations of facial expressions and body posture such as boredom, distress or worry in social settings.

These situations are hard or even impossible for Autists to deal with, they cannot break out of themselves no matter how hard they try; however, as this book will show, it is often possible, with effort, to break into the world of the Autistic. It is akin to deep-mining for gold and then finding it, an experience which can be deeply rewarding (and in the right circumstances, romantic) for everyone involved. I am sure many readers will identify with that experience, Autists are special indeed.

Autists are people who are definably different from the majority in some well understood and quantifiable ways. The number and types of these ways lie within The Autistic Spectrum, hence Autistic Spectrum Disorders (ASD). Its symptomatic presentations are many and rated "mild", "moderate", "severe" or "profound", according to their degree of influence on the functionality of the person and the likelihood of their impact on others.

Several of the conditions listed in the spectrum are well known e.g. Dyslexia, derived from the Greek "dys" meaning "bad", and "lexia", "words". Dyscalculia has the same root, but refers to numbers. Among other presentations on the spectrum are Attention Deficit Disorder, (ADD) Attention Deficit Hyperactive Disorder (ADHD) Asperger's Syndrome, (AS), Pervasive Developmental Disorders-Not Otherwise Specified (PDD-NOS), Williams Syndrome, Hyperlexia, Dyspraxia, High Function Autism, Crohn's Disease and many more. Hyperlexia is an especially adroit fluency and ability with words, written or spoken, a gift many writers, actors and politicians possess, including the Pulitzer Prize-winning Washington

Post music critic, Tim Page. Hyperlexia is found most notably in Asperger's people, we shall use the term "Aspies" from now on to describe them. Dyspraxia means being physically uncoordinated – clumsiness and is by no means unique to Autists.

Moving on to modern times the words "autism" and "schizophrenia" were both coined around 1911 by a pioneering Swiss psychiatrist named Eugen Bleuler, having noticed "autism" as a particular sub-set of behaviors-now called a "Constellation of symptoms", common to a small minority of his group of schizophrenic patients. That was very unfortunate timing as things turned out.

Much against Dr Bleuler's intentions (he had noted equally "autism" among non-schizophrenics as well) the two conditions became inextricably linked, indeed almost synonymous in the public mind, due mainly to irresponsible and sensationalist news reporting. This has stigmatized autism by ignorantly demonizing Schizophrenia and has led to a totally unfounded and unreasonable fear of and prejudice against both groups which persists even today both within some sections of the medical and Psychiatric community and numerous people in the world outside it.

This is probably due to both the ICD and DSM (IV-4) correctly listing social dysfunction or periods of social dysfunction as one of their diagnostic criteria for both disorders. We should therefore not discount the possibly that autism and schizophrenia, although very different in nature and presentation may well be related to each other, that is, may share some of the same genes or genetic sequences, in the same way as Lemon and Lime trees are related, as members the Citrus fruit family.

For some years in psychiatry it was argued by that Asperger's was a high-functioning form of schizophrenia, then as knowledge increased from the end of the 1950's it became clear that this argument-although understandable at the time- was false and that Asperger's is somewhere inside the Autism Spectrum.

A little earlier these same types of symptoms in non-schizophrenic people had been identified by a Russian Neurologist, (A specialist in the physical and chemical structures and communication pathways of the brain) Grunya Sukerava in a book published in 1926, but she did not specifically use the term "Autism" for them. Meanwhile during the same period another Psychiatrist, Dr Emil Kraepelin working at the University of Leipzig with a mixed group of patients who exhibited many of that same "Constellations" of Symptoms published a book of his observations and theories in 1927 in which he did use the term "autism". The "Constellation" is the unique "signature cluster" of symptoms which identify a specific condition or Syndrome as clinically diagnosable.

    The next step was made in the 1940's by a child psychiatrist working at the Johns Hopkins hospital in Maryland, USA. Dr Leo Kanner who also used the term in two pioneering books to describe his subset of children who exhibited the specific autistic social and emotional traits-which incidentally he believed were caused by what he termed "Refrigerator Mothers" -those who could neither nurture nor respond emotionally appropriately to their child's emotional needs. We now know how wrong this was and it placed a lot of needless guilt on two generations of women throughout the world. Irrespectively, by the end of the 1950's the word "Autism" was widely used in psychiatric practice and its meaning regarding those specific social and emotional problems was generally accepted and understood, international observations had proved that autism was in no way a coincidence and existed independently of other conditions.

Asperger's Syndrome:

At the same time as Dr Kanner was working in America, an Austrian child specialist (Pediatrician) Hans Asperger was studying yet another group of children at the University of Vienna. He also used the term "autism" and published a major book on the subject in 1944. Concurrently he had noticed both within himself and a very small number of the boys in his care, a variation of autism; a small "Cluster" of symptoms which varied from the usual pattern- one, and this is another frequently overlooked trait of Asperger's- is that Aspies naturally speak without a lot of noticeable inflection, in either a sing-song or monotone voice. Both can make them seem either dull or disinterested, neither of which is true. To these boys he allotted extra time and study until he died in 1980, aged 74. Three years later, Asperger's Syndrome was named in his honor.

The biggest breakthrough in the understanding of autism has come from the field of genetics and didn't occur until the end of the 1970's; it was followed rapidly by studies in the late 1980's and 90's, until today the heritability of autism is an established fact.

This doesn't mean that all forms of autism are always inherited, various other reasons, one being the spontaneous mutation of genes can cause it. Spontaneous mutations happen when an unknown factor or factors cause autistic gene coding to appear in a child whose parents have no history of Autism. Some of these probable factors we will discuss later in the book.

Chapter 2

Autism should only be diagnosed by a highly qualified specialist with several years of practical and professional experience. Sadly a number of school and local authority psychiatrists and psychologists who are giving out record numbers of autism Diagnoses are neither. This is one of the reasons behind the much publicized headlines "Autism Epidemic" and stories of a 6000% rise in incidence, neither of which is accurate. In many of these cases the diagnosis is simply wrong due to the so-called "expert" being under-qualified or unsuitable to make it. Even when someone has been diagnosed as autistic, it does not mean that they are, as several other conditions can mimic-to the non-expert-the signs of autism. We shall examine some of those conditions in more detail later, but first, we should answer the question "How common is Autism?" It is thought that about ten percent of people have traces of autism and about half of those have enough to make them noticeable but not to affect their everyday lives, about 1-2% are autistic enough to be diagnosed from their symptoms being obvious enough to impact theirs and others lives according to the Autism Society of America (ASA 2002).

The principle even semi-reliable method for diagnosing Autism is a process known as "differential diagnosis" (Referred to as "DDx" by Doctors)-the slow investigation and ticking-off of symptoms common to several different possible causes, one-by-one until only the root problem remains-it is costly and time consuming, while not always right, because it is "diagnosis by exclusion" rather than one by bio-clinical tests or scanned imaging- until very recently it wasn't possible to see or test for autism. The first time this method was applied in the mental field was by Dr Kraepelin.

A proper diagnosis can only be made after an extended study of the patient on the basis of experience and the diagnostic requirements (the Constellation of symptoms) as laid down in the two internationally agreed guides' defining what constitutes any illness, plus a degree of instinct by the practitioner, particularly as psychology is not yet an exact, replicatable science in the way that physics or chemistry are and we should always bear that in mind. There are NO hard scientific tests for any mental illness in the way that there are for purely physical ones such as food poisoning or cholesterol levels, which makes having the right psychologist or diagnostician even more important-a point which cannot be overstressed.

The two leading international guides referred to are the International Classification of Diseases (ICD) compiled and updated by the World Health Organization (WHO) and covering the diagnostic criteria for all known diseases and conditions and the Diagnostic and Statistical Manual of mental disorders (DSM) published by the American Psychiatric Association (APA). Both agree broadly about autism, with the DSM IV defining it as consisting, (slightly abridged), of: (I) A total of six (or more) items from (A), (B), and (C), with at least two from (A), and one each from (B) and ©

(A) Qualitative impairment in social interaction, as manifested by at least two of the following:

1. Marked impairments in the use of multiple nonverbal behaviors such as eye-to-eye gaze, facial expression, body posture, and gestures to regulate social interaction

2. Failure to develop peer relationships appropriate to developmental level:

3. A lack of spontaneous seeking to share enjoyment, interests, or achievements with other people, (e.g., by a lack of showing, bringing, or pointing out objects of interest to other people).

4. lack of social or emotional reciprocity (note: in the description, it gives the following as examples: not actively participating in simple social play or games, preferring solitary activities, or involving others in activities only as tools or "mechanical" aids)

(B) Qualitative impairments in communication as manifested by at least one of the following:

1. Delay in, or total lack of, the development of spoken language (not accompanied by an attempt to compensate through alternative modes of communication such as a gesture or mime

2. In individuals with adequate speech, marked impairment in the ability to initiate or sustain a conversation with others

3. Stereotyped and repetitive use of language or idiosyncratic language:

4. Lack of varied, spontaneous make-believe play or social imitative play appropriate to developmental level

(C) Restricted repetitive and stereotyped patterns of behavior, interests and activities, as manifested by at least two of the following:

1. Encompassing preoccupation with one or more stereotyped and restricted patterns of interest that is abnormal either in intensity or focus

2. Apparently inflexible adherence to specific, nonfunctional routines or rituals

3. Stereotyped and repetitive motor mannerisms (e.g. hand or finger flapping or twisting, or complex whole-body movements)-"Stimming":

4. Persistent preoccupation with parts of objects

(II) Delays or abnormal functioning in at least one of the following areas, with onset prior to age 3 years:

(A) Social interaction

(B) language as used in social communication

(C) symbolic or imaginative play

(III) The disturbance is not better accounted for by Rett's Disorder or Childhood Disintegrative Disorder

Before autism can be diagnosed at least two symptoms from A to C must be present permanently and at least one from section III.

Author's Note: Rett's Disorder is a physical disease of and damage to part of the white matter in the brain; it is very rare and always genetic in origin and occurs almost exclusively in girls. The patients have noticeable physical differences from normal children, including very small heads and feet. It is very serious, life-limiting and causes extreme retardation in most cases-the child can never talk or live any kind of normal or independent life. It is virtually unrelated to autism, although profound autism can closely resemble it in its lack of mental development.

Childhood Disintegrative Disorder (CDD) better known as Heller's Syndrome after Theodore Heller who first described it in 1908. In it the child affected develops normally or even super-normally until somewhere between two and ten years of age and then rapidly regresses to severe retardation from which there is no recovery. It is "Idiopathic" meaning there is no known cause. Like Rett's it can, at certain points in the regression process resemble autism, but it is not, although worryingly that has not stopped a lot of children with CDD being burdened with the wrong diagnosis and the wrong treatment and that applies equally to Rett's sufferers and their carers.

The big problem for many children with autism and other developmental conditions is that they stop progressing mentally at a certain age, if that is very young, they will remain babies in terms of mental, if not physical capability all their lives and can never communicate or take care of themselves, they cannot for example, eat, dress or use a bathroom independently. The heartbreak for the parents of such children is agonizing beyond any power of description and they need every possible support, physical, financial and emotional-as do any other "normal" siblings in the family structure. Autism is not a curse, nor is it a Judgment, it is a lottery.

The ICD (Section 10) criteria for an autism diagnosis (slightly abridged) are:

Abnormal or impaired development is evident before the age of 3 years in at least one of the following areas: Receptive or expressive language as used in social communication; The development of selective social attachments or of reciprocal social interaction; such as functional or symbolic play:

A total of at least six symptoms from (1), (2) and (3) must be present, with at least two from (1) and at least one from each of (2) and (3) for a diagnosis. Qualitative impairment in social interaction are manifested in at least two of the following areas: Failure adequately to use eye-to-eye gaze, facial expression, body postures, and gestures to regulate social Interaction; failure to develop (in a manner appropriate to mental age, and despite ample opportunities) peer relationships that involve a mutual sharing of interests, activities and emotions:

Lack of socio-emotional reciprocity is shown by an impaired or deviant response to other people's emotions; or lack of modulation of behavior according to social context; or a weak integration of social, emotional, and communicative behaviors; lack of spontaneous seeking to share enjoyment, interests, or achievements with other people (e.g. a lack of showing, bringing, or pointing out to other people objects of interest to the individual).

Qualitative abnormalities in communication as manifest in at least one of the following areas:

Delay in or total lack of, development of spoken language that is not accompanied by an attempt to compensate through the use of gestures or mime as an alternative mode of communication (often preceded by a lack of communicative babbling); Author's Note-"Baby Talk". Relative failure to initiate or sustain conversational interchange (at whatever level of language skill is present), in which there is reciprocal responsiveness to the communications of the other person: Stereotyped and repetitive use of language or idiosyncratic use of words or phrases; lack of varied spontaneous make-believe play or (when young) social imitative play

Restricted, repetitive, and stereotyped patterns of behavior, interests, and activities are manifested in at least one of the following: An encompassing preoccupation with one or more stereotyped and restricted patterns of interest that are abnormal in content or focus; or one or more interests that are abnormal in their intensity and circumscribed nature though not in their content or focus; Apparently compulsive adherence to specific, nonfunctional routines or rituals;

Author's note: Stacking blocks or other specific object arrangement, such as clothes in a particular drawer or order, which if disturbed causes the person of any age great and prolonged distress are examples of such rituals. Stereotyped and repetitive motor mannerisms that involve either hand or finger flapping or twisting or complex whole body movements...

Author's Note-these movements (Body movements are called "Motor function" by Doctors) are now known as "stimming" and are usually compulsive, life-long and often done unconsciously and/or involuntarily. It is my belief from years of research and observation that Tourette's Syndrome is part of the autistic family as a verbal form of stimming and that both, along with Obsessive-Compulsive behaviors are greatly magnified by the high levels of well- justified and grounded anxiety (anxiety makes anything worse) which is in almost all cases clearly a product of that person's life situation, in the same way as stammering and facial tics often are- much of it is the fault of the poor or non- care and concern that Autists generally receive from society and not so much of the autism itself nor any psychological disorder.Intense preoccupations with part-objects of non-functional elements of play materials (such as their order, the feel of their surface, or the vibration they generate).

The clinical picture is not attributable to the other varieties of pervasive developmental disorders; specific development disorder of Receptive language with secondary socio-emotional problems, reactive attachment disorder or dis-inhibited attachment disorder (Author's note-this means the child' physical/emotional environment). Mental retardation with some associated emotional or behavioral disorders; schizophrenia of unusually early onset; and Rett's Syndrome:

As can be seen, they are both very similar in emphasis and give together a very full picture of autistic behaviors and traits- namely of someone "living in their head" and taking little if any interest in the people or world outside to a noticeable extent-even to the point where-and this has to be said- the person, whether an adult or child is so "Frozen" and withdrawn that they need lifelong institutional care-it depends on the type and severity of the autism. It also illustrates the process of DDx.

Autistic Fact: As both children and adults Autists frequently reject both contact and gifts from family and friends, which can cause feelings of failure and alienation, particularly to parents. This behavior is not a rejection, Autists by-and-large don't like being touched and may refuse cuddles and hugs-because they are very sensitive to them- it may be constricting or even painful. With regard to presents-essentially expressions of love- they will either totally get into the Autist's world or not at all, it's not personal, they do love you, so don't be hurt by it. It's just a fact of the condition. Conversely if a toy, even one simple trinket or piece of material really "locks" the Autist's interest, it can become a lifelong talisman-very satisfying for the giver. Some you win, some you lose ☺. None of this means that a person's quality of life cannot be improved by the strategies we shall come to examine, regardless of the setting in which they are practiced.

Yet things are not quite so cut and dried as was thought when those manuals were written and approved, more than two decades ago. Researches in the fields of bio-medicine, biophysics and genetics have opened up exciting new questions and answers which have necessitated both substantial re-thinking and updating of both which adds a further imperative to finding the right diagnosis and the best therapies.

Chapter 3

What is Asperger's Syndrome?

Asperger's Syndrome (AS) is a branch of the Autism Spectrum, sharing many of its characteristics as well as those with other identifiable conditions like Schizophrenia but also with its own unique indications, making it a separate condition, as shown in the "illustrations section". The DSM (IV) lists the criteria for Asperger's Syndrome (AS) as:

Qualitative impairment in social interaction, as manifested by at least two of the following:

(A) Marked impairments in the use of multiple nonverbal behaviors such as eye-to-eye gaze, facial expression, body posture, and gestures to regulate social interaction.

B) Failure to develop peer relationships appropriate to developmental level

(C) A lack of spontaneous seeking to share enjoyment, interest or achievements with other people, (e.g. by a lack of showing, bringing, or pointing out objects of interest to other people)

(D) Lack of social or emotional reciprocity (Author's note-social give-and-take)

II Restricted repetitive & stereotyped patterns of behavior, interests and activities, as manifested by at least one of the following:

A) Encompassing preoccupation with one or more stereotyped and Restricted patterns of interest that is abnormal either in intensity or focus.

B) Apparently inflexible adherence to specific, nonfunctional routines\or rituals.

(C) Stereotyped and repetitive motor mannerisms (e.g. hand or finger-flapping or twisting (again) complex whole-body movements)

(D) Persistent preoccupation with parts of objects (Like watch mechanisms-author).

(III)The disturbance causes clinically significant impairments in social, occupational, or other important areas of functioning.

(IV) There is no clinically significant general delay in language (E.G. single words used by age 2 years, communicative phrases used by age 3 Years) there is no clinically significant delay in cognitive development or in the development of age-appropriate self-help skills, adaptive behavior (other than in social interaction) and curiosity about the environment in childhood.

Author's Note: "Cognitive" just means the ability to think and understand here. Criteria are not met for another specific Pervasive Developmental Disorder or Schizophrenia.

And by the ICD as:

A lack of any clinically significant general delay in spoken or receptive language or cognitive development: Diagnosis requires that single words should have developed by two years of age or earlier and that communicative phrases are used by three years of age or earlier. Self-help skills, adaptive behavior and curiosity about the environment during the first three years should be at a level consistent with intellectual development. However, motor milestones may be somewhat delayed and motor clumsiness is usual (although not a necessary diagnostic feature). Isolated special skills, often related to abnormal preoccupations, are common, but are not required for diagnosis (I didn't speak until 23 months, quite significantly late, the usual being 12-18 months, but as my Mum said "once you did, we couldn't stop you".

B. Qualitative abnormalities in reciprocal social interaction (criteria as for autism).

C **An unusually intense** (Author's bolding and sizing) circumscribed interest or restrictive, repetitive, and stereotyped patterns of behavior, interests and activities (criteria as for autism; however, it would be less usual for these to include either motor mannerisms or preoccupations with part-objects or non-functional elements of play materials). (Author's note, I used to love taking mechanical toys, watches, locks and small electric motors apart as a kid).

D The disorder is not attributable to other varieties of pervasive developmental disorder; schizoid-type disorder, simple schizophrenia; reactive and disinhibited attachment disorder of childhood (F94.1 and .2);

Obsessional personality disorder (OPD) or obsessive-compulsive disorder (OCD).

(Author's note: "Attributable" is a matter of personal opinion, not hard science and is therefore too subjective to be generally reliable. It is always worth seeking more than one opinion as these may vary considerably in quality and helpfulness, as well as accuracy.

These two guides however, along with the professional communities remain very much in baseline agreement as do the other manuals which follow their lead, in their agreement that these two (Autism and AS) are separate, yet closely related conditions.

However, there is one caveat; the DSM IV used today is currently in its Fourth version. Version Five has been compiled for release in May 2013 and is viewed by some, especially in Europe with deep suspicion as placing a political agenda ahead of its clinical duty and for the fact that it is composed by only ONE profession, it is not multidisciplinary as the ICD is and therefore not comprehensive or externally-checked for error. By others it is still held in high regard. The ICD is due for its Eleventh revision sometime in the middle of 2015. It has always has been updated more frequently than the DSM and being an independent global resource in its referencing, has always been my diagnostic manual of choice.

Case Study 1: We have noticed that one of the many factors uniting Autism and AS is the concentration on, and love of, repetitive behavior-which doesn't have to be a bad thing- as this case illustrates. An ADD client of mine works in the critical field of large-structure shot-blasting and painting in harsh environments. It is a highly skilled, highly detailed task.

For example, the humidity has to be EXACTLY right and needs very sensitive electronic measurement or the protective paint will not stick. It is also very repetitive, repainting the same structures is an un-ending (if well paid) task, which demands immense and purposeful concentration, as one tiny "miss", a micron or two of paint too thin could lead directly to the entire assembly being fatally weakened and hundreds, perhaps thousands of deaths. He enjoys exactly that kind of environment with no "hands-on" supervision, no set hours and total attention to detail with precise repetition, for him being an Autist makes him perfect for that job-and us a lot safer.

What is so special about AS?

The answer to that now commonly asked question is very complex, to begin with we must look both outside and behind the dry academic covers of the DSM and ICD to reveal the first, hidden secrets of Autism and AS. Firstly it needs to be remembered that overt autism is very uncommon, only that previously mentioned 1-2%. One of the few aspects of autism which is appealing is that statistic: it remains a constant throughout every country, racial, cultural and social grouping so far examined. The fact alone of autism existing is one of the defining proofs of all our shared humanity and hopefully banishes once and for all the thoughts or acts of racial bias or so-called "cultural or social superiority," which are still seen and heard today.

The number of true, full-blown Aspies is a subject of open debate and on-going study, so a single defining figure is not yet possible. My researches over more than 20 years suggest a figure of around one in about seventeen or eighteen hundred people. These people have certain differences from other autistics, as well as much in tandem with them. Firstly, because an Aspie is in most cases physically and developmentally normal-although they quite often learn to speak and co-ordinate a little later than the average child-they are not otherwise obviously abnormal-except, as the books say, that they do not have the standard social skills (or sometimes any) and responses or understanding of them. They live outside the mainstream social box. Asperger's Syndrome is- to a large apparent extent- a SOCIAL disorder, without intellectual impairment-and that is our first secret, additionally, an Aspie may (not always) have some very special talent.

Another myth surrounding autism which needs to be dispelled is that Autists are anti- or asocial. One of the things which makes autism/AS so hard for a person- I never use the term "sufferer" in referring to Autism/AS because they are not diseases- is that difficulty with social life, it's hard to make friends and form other deep relationships, even with parents and close family members due to that "closed in-ness".

That secretiveness and reclusiveness alienates the world. Autists are often perceived as shy, sly, arrogant, aloof, or simply detached and uncaring and as a result are denied the opportunities to become a part of an organization, society, group or whatever. They are adrift, often painfully alone and unable to use whatever talents they possess to benefit and contribute to society-a thing which every single one I have met desperately wants to do- to fit in and to help (We are not lazy) to love and be loved, they want to be seen, accepted and recognized for who they are, not side-lined, for what they are. In the matter of close interpersonal relationships, Autists can't recognize another person's interest in them-they need to be told-and find it hard to "reach out" appropriately, socially, sexually and intellectually. As a result they are frequently mistrusted and friendless, almost "invisible" and denied that of which the Roman philosopher, Statesman, and Lawyer, Cicero wrote of friendship two thousand years ago:

"What is sweeter than to have someone with whom you may dare discuss anything, as if communing with your own self...Adversity would indeed be hard to bear without him to whom the burden would be heavier than to oneself".

Having an autistic child makes life hard on the family, who also get pushed away and ignored by a mainstream society which cannot handle autism. For this reason I cannot speak too highly or warmly of all the largely voluntary self-help and support groups which have grown up over the last twenty years. Autism is a heavy and often solitary burden at any age. Little secret number two: Aspies can often be spotted by the way they dress-they like loose-fitting, soft clothing, brushed cotton for example and tend to go for high neck clothes-men and women alike, with a preference for light, monochrome pastel colours. Aspies are different. Across a large sample of any randomly chosen group, people with AS are, on average 10% more intelligent than their peers. The average person has an IQ of 100, the average Aspie has an IQ of about 110-the same applies across the whole range of intelligence-also their Verbal I Q -the ability to put thoughts into words-is higher again. This does not mean of course that all Aspies are geniuses, some profoundly affected ones have very low IQ's-perhaps only 70, which is a severe disability, but across the board they are smarter and talk/write better than the average-which can cause a jealousy reaction among their peers, often leading to bullying in schools, hospitals and workplaces.

It is for this reason that Aspie children are often teased as "little professors", a term originally used of them by Dr Asperger himself (and of myself by classmates and teachers, since about the age of 6) which is a very isolating and disturbing, giving an "I don't fit anywhere" experience which has left a mark. Most autistic people have been emotionally damaged in some shape or form. It is related to their extraordinary capacity to absorb, memorize process and relay information about the topics which interest them, coupled with the extreme ability to "shut the world out" and focus deeply on those topics. For example, of the small group of Aspies Dr Asperger concentrated upon, one became a Professor of Astronomy and corrected a mathematical error made by Sir Isaac Newton after 300 years and a second won the Nobel Prize for.......Literature.

Several highly respected authorities have stated that there are advantages to the individual in being autistic at certain High Function Levels, especially in being Asperger's which is widely regarded as the "mildest" form of the Autistic Spectrum Disorders. The most notable among them is perhaps the 2002 Nobel prize-winning economist, Dr Vernon Smith, currently Professor of Economics and Law at George Mason University, Fairfax, Virginia, USA. Rather than putting it as an appendix or summarizing, it is worth quoting at some length an interview given by Dr Smith to

CBNC, an American Television Channel in 2003. It helps contextualize part of the motivation for this work: namely, an attempt to delve more deeply into both the socio-economics and the many ambiguities underpinning Autism- the gap between the autistic's self-perception and the perception of them held by others.

Preamble: People with Asperger's often have extreme difficulty interacting socially, preferring to focus on narrow fields of interest. But often they're able to pursue those interests with great intensity…CBNC

Smith: "I can switch out and go into a concentrated mode and the world is completely shut out…If I'm writing something, nothing else exists… Perhaps even more importantly, I don't have any trouble thinking outside the box. I don't feel any social pressure to do things the way other people are doing them, professionally. And so I have been more open to different ways of looking at a lot of the problems in economics."

CNBC: Did you feel like you seemed strange in the eyes of other people?

Smith: Oh, yes.

CNBC: How so?

Smith: Sometimes I'm described as "not there" in a social situation. You know a social situation that lasts for a couple of hours I find it to be a tremendous amount of strain, so I've been known just to go to bed and read.

Dr Smith's wife has described him as follows: "I could not understand why he cannot be any part of my emotional world. He might not always know what he feels…In fact, many times he doesn't. He'll say, 'I don't know. What do you mean? …

Many people don't understand Vernon and they conclude wrongly about him."

This conversational evidence illuminates a crucial point about a major diagnostic criterion; that Asperger's really is primarily a cognitive, social disorder as Dr Brosnan et al of Bath University in the UK stated in the Journal of Child Psychology and Psychiatry in 2004.

Maybe that is not such an issue for a wealthy, prize-winning economist; however in my experience autism has more downsides than up. Two points in particular that arise from the interview are worth noting. It illustrates the gulf between Dr Smith's self-image – that even though he's different, it is, by his own implication all to the good- and that which others have of him, i.e. : that he is "Strange". Indeed AS is referred to in street slang as "Strange man syndrome". Aspies are certainly individualists who best march to the beat of their own drum and are always happiest and most successful when accorded the freedom to do so.

Secondly, Mrs. Smith's highly astute comment concerning people drawing the wrong conclusions about him sums up the experience of most Aspies well, as does that frequently echoed word "strange". We are often misunderstood. It is in part this "strangeness" that can and does lead to the shunning, being ignored, bullying, abuse and persecution of autistic people and their families by mainstream society-those whom Autists call "NTs", meaning "Neuro-Typicals". To guard against the ignorant few, all Autists should learn a martial art, not only for fitness and self-defense but for the extra self-confidence, philosophy and self-discipline which are learned along with them, Tae-Kwon-Do was my choice.

CNBC: Some doctors who treat people with Aspergers like Dr. Ami Klin at Yale University... (Have a different perspective) "Dr Smith's success is not typical of most people with this disability. The vast majority of individuals with Asperger Syndrome need help — without that help they won't be able to do very well... "The individuals that I know have to overcome a great deal of difficulty to maximize their potential and get the things in life they deserve", Says Dr Klin.

Dr Smith is, of course right, proven not only by his own remarkable story, but by other notable Aspie and Autistic high-achievers. Furthermore, an important and wide-ranging research project headed by Dr Larry Cahill in 2006 from the University of

California in Irvine, showed that people who have unusually large development in certain sectors of the brain, particularly the Left temporoparietal junction region have exceptional memory capacity and recall. Interestingly that same development is also associated with OCD (Obsessional Compulsive Disorder), an acknowledged member of the Autism Spectrum and is also common with Aspies.

That said; my own day-to-day knowledge and life experience and that of most autistic/AS people agrees far more closely with Dr Klin's view than it does with Dr Smith's. Being an Aspie is generally not great fun, mainly due to the interpersonal relationship issues and discrimination pain already discussed which tends to go with it, as well as the lack of help and empathy, because we look pretty "normal".

The question of whether the reason for that is clinical or societal is not yet resolved, but the majority of my clients and friends feel that if autism/AS had been a seasonal gift, like a birthday or Christmas present, they would have hoped it came with the receipt; so they could exchange it for something they actually want! ...Oh well.

At this point let's pause and take a look at another false assumption made by certain sections of the mass media and medical/education professionals; namely that so-called HFA (High Functioning Autism) and Asperger's Syndrome have the same meaning-they don't! It is not true to say that all HFAs are not Aspies nor that all Aspies are HFAs as we have seen. A radical modern re-definition of HFA is urgently needed.

"HFA is now only the correct term to apply to child or adult who has previously been diagnosed with any Autism Spectrum Disorder and additionally exhibits a Performance IQ of over 130", (HALE, 2008). The use of the term "Performance IQ" is an intentional reference to Professor Howard Gardner's (From Harvard University, USA) Theory of Multiple Intelligences (1983), a brilliant and ground-breaking work on intelligence, child potential and education. We need this definition otherwise there is the assumption that all Asperger's people are intellectually "gifted", which is not always the case.

Some with AS do have special abilities, occasionally far beyond the normal, yet those abilities are often not traditionally academic ones. It does a child a great and permanent disservice to assume ability where none exists and to expect a performance level of which the child may simply not be capable. This will lead to low self-esteem, de-motivation, adult depression and possibly self-destruction. It is a grim fact, but one which should not be avoided or made taboo; that autistics in general and Aspies in particular are substantially more likely to commit suicide than the average member of whichever society in which they live. With reference to Performance IQ: The following scale is widely used (as are others) 110-130 = "bright" 130-150 = "gifted" 150-170 = "genius" 170 + = "hyper-genius", 200+ "Super-genius".

With these facts in mind, we should be aware that even the most up-to-date of modern IQ tests are still short of being a perfectly honed and proven scientific practice, we would be wise not to place all our faith in them, despite their constant development and improvement giving us an increasingly accurate picture, especially in combination with Psychometric (Personality testing, assessing various strengths and weaknesses and very accurate these days) and Psychiatric assessment.

What is now well understood is that there is a strong inherited component to IQ, as evidenced by the work of Professor

Paul Thompson of the University of California in Los Angeles (UCLA) published in 2012. There are "smart families". Regardless of that though, it is also important to keep in mind a moral perspective as well. Because a person has a low IQ by today's criteria does not in the least diminish their value as a human being, nor does it necessarily mean their life will be empty, unhappy or unproductive unless their society makes it so. That comment applies equally to those at the opposite end of the scale, whom society tends to mistrust or fear because they are too "different", leaving them without the physical and emotional support that they so badly need, as Dr Klin noted.

    Those geniuses whether autistic or NT are very rare, but when they do occur, the Aspie/ Autist type, like Dr Smith and others seem to have, by precedent that little extra spark of insightfulness and original thinking born of that ability to focus so intently on whatever they are doing and think without socially constructed preconceptions- outside the box. It seems to give them an edge over the rest, perhaps that edge is what society calls "creativity"? None of this is intended to imply that HFAs are the only members of the Autistic Family who can excel in some way. There are many "Gifted

Autistics" who are not HFA and whose gifts reside beyond the purely intellectual, like mathematics or economics, but perhaps are in sculpture, mechanics, crafts, electronics, sports or painting, these being six well-recognized areas in which some Autists, whether Aspies or not, have done exceptionally well. There are of course geniuses in every field who are not in the slightest bit autistic: but to paraphrase a well-known Autism Community joke, "you don't have to be autistic to be a genius-but it does help.....sometimes" ☺.

Aspie Fact: myth-Aspies don't have a sense of humor. Most of us do, if only as a defense mechanism and a medium of stress relief. A few NTs find Aspie humor too clever, ironic or inappropriate in certain situations, which can cause problems, as can the fact that we don't laugh or smile much and sometimes find it hard to understand and appreciate sarcasm and jokes centering on words or phrases having double-meanings. The message to that kind of NTs is "Take a good look at you first"!

No doubt some will disagree about Dyslexia having been included without caveat earlier, in the Autistic Spectrum, when it is generally classed as a Non-Verbal Learning Disability (NLD) which although they may present in Autists, may not be Autistic in origin.

The reason behind this inclusion is that I have never met anyone with Asperger's or HFA who does not present at the same time some level of Dyslexia as well. Nor have I found any one of those two with just a single tell-tale Autistic characteristic, usually there is the main defining one, with at least two additional sub-characteristics of varying severity For example, AS plus some degree of ADHD, and/or Dyslexia and so on. In most professionals' opinion, Dyslexia can be either purely autistic or NLD in origin. Everyone involved in educational assessment should guard against an over-hasty Dyslexia-only diagnosis and should look for Autistic characteristics as well as possible visual or hearing impairments as the underlying cause. It is all too easy to be presented with apparent Dyslexia and look no farther.

      Throughout my career to date, on a number of occasions I have interviewed students who came with a Dyslexia "Statement of Needs", only to notice that ADHD or ADD were also present, making them much more likely to be Autistic than NLD. This omission will usually have a profoundly negative effect on their educational experience and standard. And, we must recognize that in certain countries schools get extra money for each dyslexic pupil-leading often to an unhealthy and unprofessional relationship between the school, the Board of Governors, the funding agency and the education psychologist-I have witnessed this systemic corruption in operation and seen children falsely "labeled" for life. It makes me very angry.

It should be a matter of the gravest concern that so many Autists have passed through education systems un-noticed due to an uninformed or incomplete diagnosis of Dyslexia as an NLD. Sometimes the two are hard to tell apart, that does not making failing to do so any more acceptable.

Now let's correct another damaging myth about Autism, namely that people with Asperger's Syndrome and indeed Schizophrenia are more dangerous than the average member of the public and are more likely to commit violent crime. Totally false: That is the conclusion of a major project, Dispelling the Stigma of Schizophrenia: By David L. Penn, Samatha Kommana, Maureen Mansfield, and Bruce Q. Link, published in the Schizophrenia Bulletin, Vol. 25, No. 3, 1999.

"People often fear individuals with schizophrenia because they believe that the disorder is linked to violent behavior. However, the research concluded that there is only a weak association between major psychiatric disorders and violence in the community. Furthermore, recent studies suggest that individuals who abuse drugs or alcohol are more prone to violence than individuals with schizophrenia. Specifically, the prevalence of violence is highest among individuals who abuse drugs (34.7%)". Numerous other projects before and since back up this team's findings, not only regarding schizophrenics, but all autistics as well. Dr J W Swanson's (Of Oxford University, England) 2006 study came to a similar conclusion; virtually every study conducted has found that murder rates and other violent crimes are significantly lower among autistic/AS people than average and that the same is true of schizophrenics.

The violence delusion originated from and was then twisted by elements in the media for the sole purpose of sensationalist, profit-boosting headlines-they concentrated on the few violent crimes committed by these groups, without ever contextualizing them by giving comparative figures from other sections of the population. Secondly they omitted to acknowledge that the vast majority of violence committed by our three groups is self-harm, despite or maybe, because of the fact that Schizophrenics, like Aspies are also as, if not more intelligent and insightful than an average person. I feel confident that many people, including families, Autists, doctors, carers and teachers will agree with the view that some sections of the media should be thoroughly ashamed of themselves and their behavior over the years, which has caused so much misery to these already stigmatized and vulnerable groups.

Bluntly, society should in reality fear the violent crime of drug users; and that particularly relates to alcohol abuse. For example, a leaked, (later verified) UK Government report commissioned by Conservative MP and now Lord Chancellor and Secretary of State for Justice, Chris Grayling and published in The Daily Mail, on April 6th 2010 in an article written by the noted journalist, James Black; the figures are horrifying:

47% of all violent crimes were committed under the influence of alcohol, including domestic violence.

62% of all random unprovoked violence committed on people by total strangers was alcohol-fuelled.

36% of all jail entries were caused by alcohol-related offences-including drink-driving.

Alcohol is without any question the primary "gateway drug", that is, one which leads people on to harder illegal drugs, like Meth, crack Cocaine, PCP ("Angel Dust"), MDMA ("Molly") Ketamine or Heroin, much more so than cannabis, for example.

That was also the conclusion of several other large-scale surveys, firstly in 1985 by John Welte and Grace Barnes for the New York State University in Buffalo, another from Missouri Western State University in 2009 and finally by the world renowned Prof David Nutt of Imperial College, London in 2010. He concluded his co-authored article in the British journal, The Lancet (Founded in 1823) by saying..... "Overall, alcohol was the most harmful drug (overall harm score 72), with heroin (55) and crack cocaine (54) in second and third places".

The salient point is that the majority of people use alcohol before using any of the others, which is what makes it and not cannabis the biggest problem as the "gateway drug", aside from all the other negatives, we have seen. That said; heavy cannabis use (More than four times a week) has been repeatedly shown to reduce IQ and increase the chances of developing mental illness, especially when the users are younger, that is, teens and twenty-somethings.

The risk among older users is considerably less, leaving aside the fact that it damages memory and increases the chances of dementia in later life. There is the possibility that it could equally affect the brains of developing babies whose mothers use the drug during pregnancy, perhaps leading to autism or Learning Difficulties. That is so far unproven, however my message is strongly, "don't take that chance".

Society needs to look long and hard at its real and not imagined threats, primarily alcohol, but also the highly stimulant mind-altering drugs that include Cocaine and Meth-amphetamines as the causes of serious crime and stop the witch-hunting of those who are already themselves innocent victims of certain, mainly harmless, if obvious mental conditions. A prime message of this book is, "please look at the facts first-not the trash end of the media- before making judgments about Autism in particular or mental health in general" (Hale). An Aspie friend put it rightly when she said to me, "I don't have a problem with being Asperger's, there's other people have a problem with me being Asperger's".

Chapter 4

The Significance of Autism/Asperger's Syndrome:

We need to begin this chapter with a re-cap of how Autism is diagnosed: Briefly if anyone at any age exhibits sufficient of the criteria unique to autism, as defined by the ICD and DSM IV then the correct diagnosis is "autism" once other potential causes have been ruled out. The patient can then, according to which and to how big an extent he/she has their symptoms, be told exactly which autistic condition or conditions they have where they are in the Autistic Family and therefore find the most appropriate help-at least that's how the system is supposed to work.

But...Autism has two faces, dependent (usually) on its likely cause and defined largely by the age at which it presents-that is - becomes noticeable to the parents and a doctor-the point where it is clear that the child is "different". In practice, someone especially close to the child, usually the mother will instinctively know her baby is different much earlier than the three years cited in the manuals. My Mum noticed before I was two.

There are, fundamentally, two distinct versions of autism: I call one "Classical Autism", the cause of which is wholly genetic and is always apparent before the age of three, as both the DSM IV and ICD agree. The second type is best explained in Sue Thompson's excellent (1996) book The Source for Non-Verbal Learning Disorders (NLDs). Not only is it an invaluable practical manual (and highly recommended from the author's own experience for SEN teachers and carers alike) it also explains concisely both the nature of NLDs and the underlying science behind the conditions which separates them from genetically induced childhood autism. She explains during the course of the book, how some children, (and adults) develop autistic symptomology for very specific reasons which we shall examine in the next chapter, across the whole age range.

These cases are usually referred to as Non-Verbal Learning Disorders to distinguish them from inherited "classical" autism. Sometimes the two are impossible to tell apart, except (and then not always) by genetic testing and CT/ (f) MRI scanning, because although the causes are different, the observable effects are often very similar.

To complicate things a little further: (That sentence itself would serve as an appropriate motto for dealing with autism), children without autistic genes can be exposed to the other causes of autism before the age of three. Again without genetic testing such children may be classed as having classical autism, which is medically incurable, but NOT untreatable, rather than being recognized as NLD autistic, which with some patients by removing the cause(s) can be virtually cured and the child or adult go on to live a relatively normal life if it is caught early enough. It is not possible to over-emphasize the VITAL importance of the earliest possible diagnosis for all autistics for this and numerous other reasons, which we shall consider later.

Autism/NLD: What's the difference?

On the face of it there is usually little apparent difference in outward symptomology between individuals from either group: Anything from mild Dyslexia only, to deep, perhaps non-verbal retardation requiring constant care in all ways. Principally, NLD causes and signs are more often to be found in various parts of the right side of the brain, although no one is too sure why.

Classical autism, in stark contrast is predominantly located in the left and front parts of the brain and principally acquired through the parents' germ-lines- and those trends run through families. Thus, when attempting to diagnose either, the specialist must take a detailed family history. The functionality affected can differ significantly from NLD. This core difference has become much clearer recently, at least in part due to the technical advances in diagnosis we have mentioned. However this equipment is far from universally available and a large number of professionals around the world still have to rely on Dr Kraepelin's Differential Diagnostic method:

As so often though in science there is another unexplained anomaly. That is; a prime Diagnostic presentation for NLD is a substantial gap between Performance IQ and Verbal IQ, the latter being by far the higher. That is also the first diagnostic criterion for Asperger's. However no practitioner should diagnose from one symptom alone in any discipline. There is though, yet more to

Classical Autism: The actual physical and chemical structure of the brain is different from ordinary people; an extra development, especially in the left and frontal lobes of the brain is often found in AS people. This may be where any superior function arises. The left brain is associated with mathematical, logic and language skills, the right more with spatial perception and art, which will be different from the normal left/right proportions, affecting the autistic's physical, emotional and intellectual experience of the world.

Autistics literally see and feel the world in a totally different way from NTs. That is why they are often said to "be in a world of their own". They are! From this comes the frequent refrain from people that Autistics seem "elsewhere", in "dreamland", or "Head in the clouds". Or perhaps, thinking of Newton in the Stars? From those with extra right frontal development as well as left, the artistic ability- even genius, the clearest examples of how that works in practice may lie in the paintings of the Dutch artists Vincent Van Gogh and Jan Vermeer, both Autistic geniuses with the added ability to paint the world not only as they saw it, but as they felt it.

Naturally from this spatial imbalance we see also one of the roots of Autistic Dyslexia. Another is short-term memory problems, forgetting where they put the car or house keys. One reason this may happen is that "their mind is working so fast; it has started on a new task before completing and remembering the current one" (Hale). That is one of many possible explanations of ADD (Attention Deficit Disorder) it itself an associated presentation common to most Dyslexics, literally the word in the brain is partially forgotten and therefore incomplete before its full message reaches the hand. With writing the process is reversed, the brain has moved on to the next word(s) before completing the current one.

Autistic Fact: Some Autists repeat, especially when excited the last word of any sentence they are speaking or writing, quite unconsciously.

To sum up: NLD is due to brain damage of varying nature, leading to some retardation of varying severity and is not present at birth. Classical Autism is due to a different, inherited brain structure, which (McWilliams, 1999 C W 6th Edition: Treatment Form Formulary: Volume VIII) can result in anything from severe retardation to extraordinary abilities and is always incipient from birth, perhaps appearing immediately or sometimes requiring a "trigger", but always appearing before the age of three. The fact is;

there is still a great deal about the brain we do not know and we do not have a clear idea of how it works. Now that nearly every day new research around the world is shedding increasing light on this complex subject and resolving some of the apparent paradoxes and gaps within the current theories, we can reasonably hope for great progress and increasingly better understanding and treatments for all forms of Autism within the next few years.

There is also another form NLD that can also cause autism- which to differentiate it is called NSLD-Non-Specific Learning Difficulty, which has much the same symptoms as autism and NLD, but no agreed cause(s) can be found. Almost everything in this book applies equally to people with an NSLD and to their caregivers/teachers.

Williams' Syndrome (WS):

The results of Williams' Syndrome are far -reaching and sadly incurable. There are many, but to list a few; Williamsonians have very friendly, out-going and trusting personalities-like a lot of Autists- but are usually retarded to a greater or lesser degree- along clearly autistic lines-and many cannot live their lives unassisted. Typically they tend to be shorter and slimmer than the average. They have characteristically thin, sharply defined, almost pixie or Hobbit-like faces and engaging smiles. Lots of them are especially articulate public and private speakers and charming to know. The majority are very musical and lots have "perfect pitch" and like many other autistics have an above average tendency to be left-handed, left-footed and left-eye dominant. Virtually all autistics have a special talent of some kind(s), regardless of IQ. Some Williams' people have IQ's of only 60, compared with the average of 100, but they still retain the same lovely, open and warm personality along with their other qualities. This again shows how a person's worth can and should not be measured by their IQ alone and that is another strong message that needs to be shouted out into the world. Unfortunately the condition also brings with it severe problems with heart function and causes a narrowing of the arteries (termed "Stenosis" by Surgeons). Williamsonians are likely to suffer heart failure and strokes and do not often live a full lifespan.

Furthermore sufferers are prone to over-store calcium which is in itself dangerous as it blocks up the cardio -vascular- system,-

the arteries and veins serving the heart and so they need to avoid Vitamin D as it increases calcium retention and calcium deposits block blood vessels. In a cruel twist of fate, this means Williams' people are very likely to suffer from MS-type (Multiple Sclerosis) symptoms which virtually mirror many of those of Vitamin D deficiency; this can lead even experienced doctors to mis-diagnose either one or both. This happens to ordinary members of the public as well-always seek a second, and third opinion on MS.

A 2009 study by Dr Jodie Barton of the University of Toronto, Canada even found that high doses of Vitamin D dramatically cut the relapse rates among her group of actual MS patients. An interesting rider to this is: a lack of maternal and subsequent embryonic Vitamins and other vital nutrients has been proposed as a cause of Autism, although-to my knowledge- there has been little research into the idea. It is based on the question that since governments began to warn people to stay out of the sun in the 1990's for fear of skin cancer-and that Vitamin D is made in the skin by the action of sunlight- our collective Vitamin D levels have dropped at about the same time as autism levels appear to have risen dramatically. As an aside, Vitamin D isn't actually a vitamin at all but an important hormone because it is made in a body organ-the skin - which wasn't understood at the time of its discovery in America in 1913, when it was originally synthesized from cod liver oil.

Perhaps the most obvious physical feature of Williams' Syndrome, (after that brief detour) certainly in milder cases is that the bridge of the nose starts much lower down the face than is normal. That is also true of the majority of Autists, but not to anything like such a marked degree.

Down's syndrome:

Down's is not an autistic condition of course, but it does share a few characteristics with some forms of Autism, retardation being one and a smaller than average head being another. Downs people like Williamsonians have that fun, charming and loving personality.

That stated, Down's syndrome is another piece of the overall picture, in that it too, like Williams' is a proven genetic condition, the cause of which is a complete or partial third copy of Chromosome 21 (we're only supposed to have two copies of each of our twenty-three pairs of chromosomes). All this aside, knowing Down's people and carers, they have all said that of the advice in this book has been highly useful and relevant to their lives, as well as to Autists. I hoped always to make this piece as inclusive as possible, especially as many of the education and social strategies later outlined are equally valid and helpful for NTs as well- of any age.

Autism and Epilepsy-is there a connection?

Since the late 1960's there have been whispers among groups of teachers and psychologists that certain "Special Education Needs" (SEN) children, in this instance, Autistic pupils, seemed more prone to seizures than other groups, there was no real evidence available, just "word of mouth". It is now possible, following a great deal of research from various groups and individuals in recent times and from across the world to reveal the answer.

That answer is categorically "Yes". About one-in-three Autists experience more than one epileptic seizure during their lifetime. (US National Library/Institutes of Health-PubMed, 2005), subsequent studies have confirmed these findings. The average epilepsy rate within the general adult population is about five people per thousand only (WHO). One seizure does not make a person an epileptic, the diagnosis requires at least three or four. This is compared with the three hundred and thirty-four per thousand for Autists, everyone was sure the two conditions must somehow be linked –but couldn't find out how-and they were right, as was finally proved by the following-the author's redact of an article published by ScienceDaily, April the 8th, 2011.

"Researchers have identified a new gene that predisposes people to both autism and epilepsy. The team led by the neurologist Dr. Patrick Cossette, found a severe mutation of the synapsin gene (SYN1) in all members of a large French-Canadian family suffering from epilepsy, including individuals also suffering from autism. This study also includes an analysis of two cohorts of individuals from Quebec, which made it possible to identify other mutations in the SYN1 gene among 1% and 3.5% of those suffering respectively from autism and epilepsy, while several carriers of the SYN1 mutation displayed symptoms of both disorders.

"The results show for the first time the role of the SYN1 gene in autism, in addition to epilepsy, and strengthen the hypothesis that a deregulation of the function of synapse because of this mutation is the cause of both diseases, until now, no other genetic study of humans has made this demonstration."

Author's Note: He also mentioned that this correlation of epilepsy and autism makes the two "co-morbid", which means that if two or more illnesses co-exist at the same time as normal occurrence-doctors know there's a connection. This is an illuminating piece of research because it irrefutably ties autism- which is broadly, but wrongly seen as purely psychiatric in nature- with one that is a very obviously purely physical in nature, although both are brain-based. This leads us to the understanding of Autism for what it truly is, a "Whole body condition". For that reason I advise all autistic/AS patients of all ages to wear a "Medic Alert" bracelet or neck-let at all times identifying their condition in case of emergency. If cost forbids that, a signed doctor's note and contact details in a plastic case will work equally well.

Imagine the sheer wretched hopelessness of having the perceived stigmas of autism AND epilepsy. To give a sharp perspective on that-it was not until 1970 that epileptics were even allowed to marry in the United Kingdom. In the developing world only one epileptic in ten ever receives treatment, not necessarily because the family is unaware of it or can't afford treatment, but because it will not admit to the community the "shame" of an epileptic son or daughter, fearing (usually correctly) it would make all their children unmarriageable. Add autism to that mix and that is what I meant about "returning the gift".

Over the years many of us have become increasingly frustrated and dissatisfied with the use of negative and prejudicial terminology towards Autists. If we pull together we can change that perception directly. Let's start with the word "Disorder", again, having its origin in that word Dys/Dis-"bad", a word which has terrible connotations of inferiority and even resonances of malice. And then "disability" and "Defect". Yes, in a substantial number of people autism does reduce their ability to function fully and happily in most societies. That we recognize. However there are those-like Dr Smith for whom it is a real superpower- not a disability. Therefore would not the term "Condition" or "State" be both more legitimate and less stigmatizing? In addition, we should all stop and think…and be very uncomfortable with some of the negative and judgmental terminology used in the field of education, both child and adult.

Even if a person's educational potential is greatly limited by one or more of these conditions we should remember three things: 1) it does not diminish their humanity, 2) it is not their "fault" and 3) that some improvement, however great or small is always possible. For these reasons, we should consider, and this guide proposes, the abandoning of such terms as NLD and other so-and-so "disorders", and replacing them with the terms Alternative Education/Employment Profiles (AEPs-Hale 2002) with the additional Descriptors of Autistic or Non- Autistic, followed by their characteristics. Then ADHD becomes "an A (autistic) AEP characterized by ...." with the client's name, and assessment. This should generate an Individual Development or Career Program (I D/CP) agreed upon between the client, a professional assessor and the carer/provider as appropriate, regardless of the client's age. It is profoundly damaging, confidence-killing and terrifying to be causally "labeled" and shoved into a convenient and unexplained dark box- for life, especially for a child. To have one's cards and future so strongly and adversely marked in advance from such a young age is a fearful experience and a violation of the most basic of human rights as well as of the human spirit.

It is also a cruelly overlooked fact that the needs and abilities of autistic adults are all-too-often under-appreciated or ignored altogether, both in society as a whole and the workplace. Autistic people have a great deal to offer, to waste that potential talent pool, may be cheap and convenient to the short -term thinking, small-minded "corporate" mentality in areas of education and employment but it is professionally, ethically, financially and morally indefensible. Fortunately, a few employers are now beginning to realize the special talents Autistic people can possess and are actively recruiting them; the German electronics company SAP being a shining example along with Vodafone and Microsoft. But these are rare shining lights.

This book will continue to use the term HFA, as it will the name AS in long overdue tribute to Dr Hans Asperger, who published his seminal paper on the subject in 1944, less than a year after Autism had first been fully described, despite the highly controversial decision of the APA to drop the actual term from its

2013 DSM-V rewrite. The symptomology of AS however remains within a larger autism section of the DSM-V.

It has also become apparent that the use of the word "spectrum" in this context, although very descriptive and upbeat with its implied relationship to a rainbow is factually somewhat misleading, as it conjures up an image of gradation, that is of each component lying neatly next to its neighbor, like the tools laid out on a carpenter's bench or items on the store shelf. As we have seen though, all the types of autism/AS are overlapping and interlocking at the deepest levels and never found in isolation, whether they are Classical or NLD in origin.

For this reason let us now replace "The Autistic Spectrum" with "The Hale Autism family tree", see illustration below, as a much more representative scientific and practical description of this complex subject, showing how autism comes in so many varieties and combinations

The Hale Autism Family Tree:

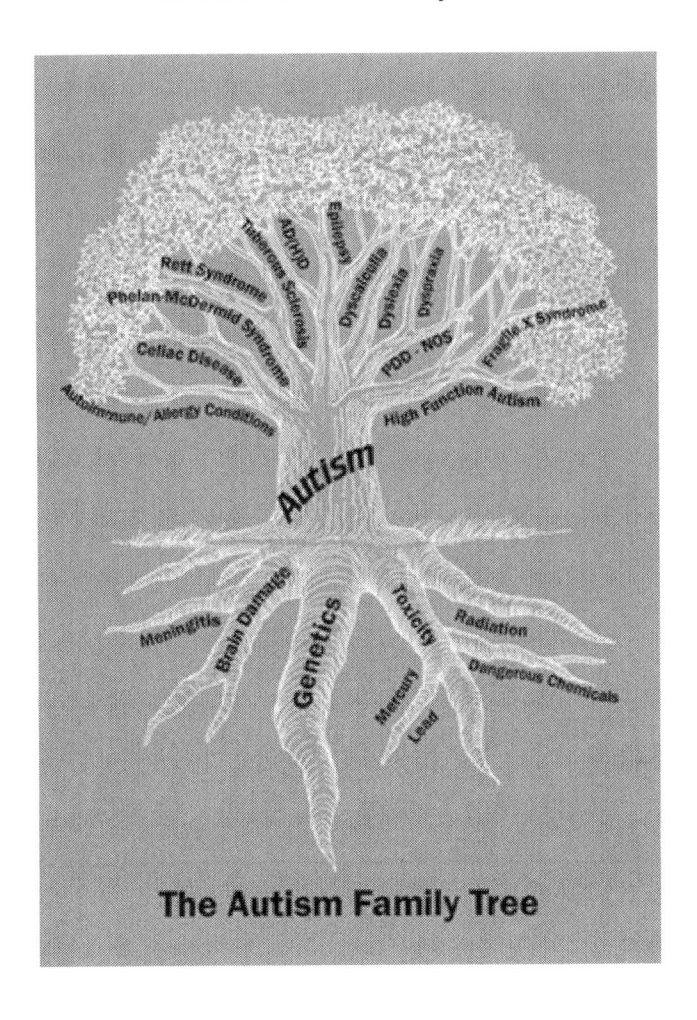

The Autism Family Tree

These are the principle conditions, sub-conditions, related branches and some of the co-morbidities which together comprise the Autism Family and are shown in the Illustrations part in this book. They include Epilepsy, Tuberos sclerosis and dyslexia. A Few more Fun Facts: Autistic/AS Comedians, Actors and musicians: Dan Ackroyd ("Ghostbusters", "The Blues Brothers"), Darryl Hannah "Mermaid", Gary Numan, Marty Balin (Jefferson Airplane), John Denver, Jim Henson (The Muppets), singer/songwriter, James Taylor, further back and significantly, both classical composers Wolfgang Mozart and Gustav Mahler.

Autism and Society-Education:

All autistic conditions bring with them an unusual gift for copying, memory and imitation which, if used correctly at the earliest possible age can be turned into a real advantage. The key to using that capacity to help the integration of the Autist more comfortably into society as a whole is the finding of and encouragement to imitate highly positive role models. Conversely, if a bad role model should be one available, it can be doubly disastrous for the over-trusting Autist. This strategy can be successful at any age, but obviously the younger the start, the better. Ideally the role models would be the parents, caregivers, siblings and other family members. Where that is not possible, Community leaders, teachers, characters in books or TV series can serve well instead. The idea is to encourage, not cajole- Autists tend to be very stubborn- the Autie to copy the model. This can start with the apparently simplest things which an NT barely notices, yet which an Autie doesn't understand at all. Things like dental and personal hygiene; both vital to good health-there is a proven link between lack of oral hygiene and heart disease, for example.

Autists aren't slovenly, but they can at times be oblivious to themselves and others. Hair care and nails are another often overlooked area. Social manners can be taught using this method, "please" "thank you", "excuse me" "how are you"? "Would you like something to eat/drink," "well done". Shaking hands, learning to look people in the eye, making small talk, all the little things, the social give-and-take (reciprocity) and politenesses that make up the everyday life of any society and which are essential for a successful and happy life in the NT world. The same is true of dress codes; what-to-wear at certain events; job interviews are an important example. As the Autist masters these foundations, more and more skills and nuances can be added. This process may seem trivial to some, but I and others have used it beneficially, it adds up and over the years and delivers lasting rewards, even though it takes a long time-and a lot of trial and error. Patience coupled with determination is the key.

Chapter 5

The main roots and theories of Autism and NLDs:

As we now understand Autism is a long established collection of a sufficient number of specific behaviors, the syndromes of which may be produced by one or more of the stimuli which we'll examine in this chapter. Firstly; TBIs as doctors call them-Traumatic Brain Injuries-a big whack on the head to the rest of us☺. They can be caused by direct blows to the head, or by being hit by a pressure wave following an explosion in one form or another. Either can result in permanent physical damage to the brain. If the damaged areas are the ones which relate to autism, the person will become autistic-period.

Savants: Tommy McHugh was a builder in Liverpool, England, a huge man with a criminal record for anti-social behavior and violence....until he suffered two brain hemorrhages after an accident in his bathroom. Surgeons struggled to save his life, finally he was discharged from hospital-a completely changed man in many ways, one of which was that he had forgotten both why and how to eat and walk, as well as his name, still he recovered. He acquired the reputation as a gentle giant from then on and began increasingly to display a brilliant and all-consuming passion for painting, of which no hint was ever present before and which became his whole life- and the source of a successful living- he had real talent and verve. The strokes occurred in 2001; after several internationally acclaimed art exhibitions, he died in 2012, aged 62.

Secondly; certain diseases: There are four basic categories of disease that can directly damage the brain like TBIs. The common one is Meningitis, which is caused by an infection of the protective membrane which encloses the brain and spine and is usually caused by one of a number of bacteria, but there are viral types as well. Encephalitis: is any infection which causes the brain itself to swell and become damaged, it is usually caused by some virus or other, Rubella is one of those as is CMV (Cytomegalovirus), one of the Herpes family, as are "cold sores". Rubella is better known as "German Measles" and can be life-threatening to young children. There are very effective vaccines against all of the above and my strong advice to any parent is to have your child vaccinated against them as early as possible.

The third category are the degenerative brain conditions, caused by the brain or its blood supply becoming clogged up, usually by plaque deposits and/or knot-like protein tangles of various descriptions. These result in parts of the brain dying over time. Parkinson's Disease (PD) and Alzheimer's Disease (AD) are two and vary only by where in the brain the plaquing occurs, as they both produce much the same tragic effects of which we're all too well aware, loss of memory, sense of smell, mobility, personality changes, speech difficulty and loss of personal and spatial awareness, among others. During the phases of both these and related conditions, strongly autistic traits will appear. Aluminum has been linked to Alzheimer's. Research published in the Journal of Applied Toxicology indicated that long-term exposure to human mammary (Breast) epithelial cells contaminated with aluminum can in some incidences result in anchorage-independent growth, a key indicator of cultured tumor cells (cancer) and of cells on the way to becoming malignant, but this is still not proven conclusively. A widely used product containing aluminum is underarm deodorant (antiperspirants); there are many others; cake mix and some suntan products being just two, again emphasizing the other hazards of toxic metals, aside from Autism.

Similarly the same Autistic presentation will happen with cerebral arteriosclerosis (CA). With this the arteries and capillaries supplying blood and oxygen to the head become increasingly narrowed and hardened by plaques and again, those parts of the brain affected, begin to wither and then stop working. If those parts are the ones which, when affected are the ones which produce autism, then again, the person will become autistic-Acquired, as distinct from Classical Autism. Fourthly if the blockages in the blood circulatory system occur to the brain spontaneously they are known as Strokes, if in the lungs, Pulmonary Embolisms and if to the heart, Heart Attacks or "Cardio-vascular events". In each event brain damage may result from lack of oxygen (Hypoxia).

The general perception of the degenerative conditions is that they affect only the seniors' age group, which is generally true. However, we should be aware that PD, AD and CA can begin as early as the 35-40 age groups and that the same is true of heart disease as well. Premature Birth and Low Birth weight: Studies in 2008 by the famous McGill Medical School in Montreal, Canada found that babies born seven to fourteen weeks too early were four times more likely to exhibit signs of autism. In 2011 a team from Pennsylvania led by Jennifer Pinto-Martin studied nearly a thousand early-borns of low weight and found they were up to five times more likely to be autistic than the average, probably due to the brain having insufficient time to develop fully. This research though begs an unanswered question' namely-"were these children born too early because they had inherited autism at conception, or did their premature birth cause their autism?

Oxygen starvation at birth can also cause all the symptoms of Autism, please check out the Pediatric team's record before choosing a birthing place. Finally, cancer (and some cancer treatments) can damage the brain and may lead to autism/NLDs presenting at any stage of life.

Environmental:

In this section we are looking at the environmental agents who can cause brain damage and lead to Non-classical Autism and NLDs, usually from birth or in young children. This whole question is under-researched and few authorities seem to actually want to conduct thorough large-scale studies, perhaps due to the pressure from corporate lobbying groups? The word for these substances is "Teratogens" and refers to any material which can cause multiple birth and growth defects in humans, other animals and plants. Among well-known ones are excessive radiation exposures to the mother, father and/or fetus. Shocking evidence for this has emerged from the cities in Japan which were nuclear bombed in 1945, Hiroshima and Nagasaki, where radiation-caused birth defects continue to stalk each new generation to this day, autism included. The lands surrounding the shattered nuclear power station at Chernobyl in the Ukraine are another high-profile example. There is also cursory and anecdotal evidence that children born near old, leaky nuclear plants and other installations, such as Sellafield, in Cumbria County in the United Kingdom, also suffer far higher levels of cancer and other health problems compared with the national average -and the existence of "childhood cancer clusters" is fairly well recorded and accepted by many people around the world.

Those stations affect the plant and animal life around them as well, whether by land, sea, air or in nearby rivers. The results are clearly visible in birth deformities to the wildlife, which, along with the local water supply finds its way into our shops and bodies. Very similar patterns of child deformity and adult sickness are still clearly to be found in Vietnam, Laos and Cambodia after the use of the defoliant chemical spray "Agent Orange" during the Vietnam War.

Diabetes during pregnancy, as well as alcohol consumption can cause birth abnormalities of numerous types, as of course can cigarette smoking. Some High Fructose Corn Syrups (HFCS) have been suggested to be harmful, so far the pharmo-clinical evidence for that has proved inconclusive. Proven Teratogens include certain Organo-based farm pesticides as shown by various tests conducted in 2005 and then by the California Department of Public Health in 2007. Similarly a survey conducted in 2011 suggests living near the fumes of a main road may damage the baby's development. The emphasis has to be on the word "may", it is not fully verified. Increasing female obesity in the Western world -being too fat- has also been shown predispose a child towards autism, it is yet another factor in the increasing rates of autism (Pediatrics: April 9th, 2012).

There are other theories; including low maternal thyroid function-all pregnant women should get a thyroid test as early in the pregnancy as possible- for their own sake as well as baby's. High household stress or depression levels, which abnormally raise levels of the hormone Cortisol (The Stress Hormone) perhaps from financial hardship seems to cause babies of below average weight to be born, but any connection to that or thyroid levels with autism/AS, is as yet, tentative at best, as is another very new theory, namely that older fathers (Defined as being over forty) are more likely to have autistic or schizophrenic offspring than those of younger ones. This though is according to a single study conducted by a team in Iceland and using a sample of only eighty-eight children.

Pre-natal exposure to some prescription medicines, as well as illegal street drugs such as solvents, Meth, Crack, LSD ("Acid") PCP (phenylcyclohexylpiperidine) and heroin are well known to damage the developing child. A class of chemicals called BPA, Bis phenol-A which leeches out of common plastic bottles, is regarded by some as dangerous, with some serious evidence to back up that claim, including an in-depth study published in The Journal of Human Reproduction, July 31, 2013, linking them with falling human fertility (and by extension, that of other creatures). The same has been found of other forms of Organo chemicals including PCBs- Polychlorinated biphenyls, used in a wide variety of products from paints to adhesives to lubricating agents and some common household electrical devices.

There is an increasing body of evidence that EMR (Electro-magnetic radiation) can cause cancer anywhere in the body, at any age including the brain. EMR has been directly blamed for the perceived rise in autism since the 1970's as our exposure to it (in the industrialized world) has increased more than sixty-times since then. EMR emitters embrace pretty much anything powered by electricity, Televisions, hairdryers, microwave ovens, cellular phones and thousands more items. Living near cellular phone masts, electricity sub-stations or high-voltage power-lines would also increase the exposure level greatly and many people who live close to these sources report serious health problems, from across the world. Children are especially vulnerable to these effects as it affects their normal growth.

There has simply not been enough research to either fully confirm or refute these ideas...but it is worth noting that in April of 2011 the WHO issued a strong warning that hand-held mobile phones are linked to a certain type of brain cancer-Glioma (from which Senator Edward Kennedy died) – based mainly on a study by their International Agency for Research on Cancer (IARC) led by Dr Jonathon Samet of the University of Southern California and on findings from the 1960's onwards conducted in Sweden. That research is ongoing and is increasingly disturbing in its implications as the data mounts up concerning over-use of mobile telephones.

NIDS: Is a new theory: it is Neuro-Immune Dysfunction Syndrome. The theory is that the autism traits are a by-product of a weakened immune system stemming from a continuous and perhaps almost un-noticeable (Asymptomatic, meaning there are no clearly visible symptoms like fever) low-level attack, normally by a virus. Again, this is unproven, but it's always worth getting a broad series of viral tests, as at least some can be cured. This wide range of tests is a "Viral panel". What is sure is that some viruses cause cancer. Hepatitis strains can cause liver cancer, as can about thirty of the hundreds of strains of the Human Papillomavirus (HPV), a common sexually transmitted virus affecting up to eight out of ten British adults and about twenty million Americans. It has been shown to produce a variety of throat and reproductive system cancers, including cervical, penile and mouth. It can be carried and transmitted by both genders.

In 2008 the United Kingdom began a vaccination program targeting girls between the ages of twelve and thirteen. Time has shown it was a good idea as it has cut infection rates dramatically, still why not target boys equally, that smacks of gender bias? HPV is of the same virus family as Cytomegalovirus (CMV) and the Epstein - Barr virus (EPV) - Mononucleosis/Glandular Fever, both of which may be the progenitors of various cancers. A virus causes cancer by inhabiting and altering the genetic structure every cell in your body, including brain cells, in doing so they cause a genetic mutation in some cells, which can then become malignant.

This genetic hijacking is the basis of another theory that autism is the result of viral infections affecting the brain structure, either before birth or shortly afterwards before the child's immune system is well developed. Once again, this is an interesting and logical idea and one which ties in well with the NIDS theory but both remain under-researched, so we cannot yet be positive one way or the other, more money for research is needed.

Lastly the increasingly well researched and funded work done by Professor Simon Baron- Cohen (Oscar-winning comedian Ali G's cousin), head of the Autism Research Centre (ARC) and his team at England's prestigious Cambridge University and probably the world's leading authority on Asperger's Syndrome. This involves the pre-birth environment- of the baby (Fetus) in the mother's womb (Uterus). He calls it the FT (Fetal Testosterone) theory. Basically he has found that some babies are exposed to higher uterine testosterone levels than others. (Testosterone is the male hormone, but all women have a small amount naturally). It seems that a few women have at times unusually high levels which affect the baby, giving it (male or female) in some areas markedly stronger (Traditionally) masculine traits, specifically with regards to perceived lack of emotional and social empathy and reciprocity, which are very Aspie characteristics.

Professor Baron-Cohen believes this is what AS actually is, and some of his supporters believe it further applies, in different degrees to other members of the autism family, notably PDD-NOS. It is broadly referred to as the "Extreme Male Brain Theory". It does not mean that such people have some kind of brutish "Caveman Complex" thing going on, far from it, but it may explain at least one aspect of the mystery of the severe social disability which Asperger's Syndrome certainly is.

It is an immensely complex bio-chemical and psychological work which is well beyond the scope of this book to detail in its entirety. Research into it continues. From it Professor Baron-Cohen has evolved his "Empathy-Systematizing Theory", which we shall explore in a later chapter. Autie/AS Myth bites the dust :-). Surprisingly, a lot of people share the belief that Autists in general and Aspies in particular are either unable or unwilling to lie or detect sarcasm and irony. This isn't at all true, except during childhood; we do lie, we sometimes edit the full truth and we can bluff very convincingly, aided by our tendency to have expressionless faces. A tip-never play poker against a skilled Aspie -unless you have lots of money to lose ☺.

What is true is that we are very literal, that is; we take words and actions entirely at face-value because we cannot understand social or vocal cues and nuances. We also tend to respond in the same very straight-forward, perhaps one-dimensional ways, so yes, naturally we are very honest and straight-talking, another personality trait which is frequently misunderstood and interpreted as hostile or rude. We are not good at shallow flattery or "small talk", some find that refreshing, more seem to find it offensive, which, not having those social skills Aspies can't understand any more than they can the consequences of their words to the point if/until they learn to self-censor in public at least.

The constant rebuttals resulting from this directness only add to the Autist's sense of alienation from mainstream society and increase their withdrawal and "closed-in-ness", a classic viscous circle. That said, life experience of the NT world quickly teaches us to dissemble or lie when we have to-it doesn't come naturally... but it does come eventually as a self-defense tactic and social self-censoring can be taught successfully using the techniques in this book. Aspie Literal true story: A friend (Aspies do have them, just not very many) asked me about a cold medicine "How did you find it"? To which I replied, not trying to be "clever", "at the chemist".

Toxicity:

Firstly, lots of poisons from household bleach to floor polish onwards can damage the body and brain including rat poison, carbon monoxide gas, Arsenic and perhaps in the case of both children and adults excess Mono-sodium-glutamate in food (it's an additive which boosts taste) is considered by many to be harmful, although the evidence is sketchy-so far. Aspartame is a clear danger; it's an artificial sweetener whose appalling side-effects have been widely posted since the 1990's. Yet along with high-energy, high-sugar drinks which have been linked to both ADHD-type symptoms and certain cancers, it is still available in confectionaries, drinks and numerous other products on every store shelf (American Journal of Clinical Medicine, December 2012). Other rare but possible culprits are a few types of mold which are known to cause brain damage, fungal meningitis being one.

This section's main focus though is on heavy metal poisoning. Almost all metals when swallowed, inhaled or absorbed through the skin are dangerous, among the worst are Silver, aluminum -the recommendation is not to cook (or drink from) in uncoated aluminum pots, foil or pans (Global Health Center) - Gold, Beryllium, Tin, Lead, Copper, Arsenic, Cadmium, Mercury, Zinc and Nickel-among others, (US Department of Labor). Generally the heavier and softer the metal, the more and quicker the damage it does, so we shall focus mainly on Lead, Mercury and Copper, three very common metals, each with proven links to autism. In all cases the amounts needed to cause serious harm can arrive suddenly in an accident, or accumulate over time. A note on Gold: The ancient tradition of a trader biting a coin or token offered by a stranger has its basis in it being soft. There will be a bite mark left on a genuine piece; no mark signified that the piece was an iron alloy counterfeit.

Copper- (Chemical symbol Cu). Probably the least reported but most common form of heavy metal poisoning. Excess copper comes from many sources, copper piping for household or industrial water supplies, copper cooking utensils, it is in virtually every electrical device and being a soft, malleable metal like gold, it is easily absorbed through the skin over extended periods. It is doubly dangerous to children, who will, by nature put virtually anything in their mouths to suck, chew or eat. Copper is also readily absorbed from copper bracelets and other jewelry. We can get it in high amounts from red meat, wheat, nuts, and shellfish, coffee, chocolate and green-leaf vegetables like lettuce- and from mushrooms. Physically; a liver disorder as well as excess from the aforementioned sources can lead to the buildup of copper in the body known as "Copper Toxicity Syndrome", (CTS) as the liver is the organ which stores and regulates copper levels. The right amount of copper is good, it promotes protein absorption, efficient energy production and healthy bones, among other things, but too much, detected by a hair, blood or eye test is very harmful.

An inherited condition in which the liver stores excess copper instead of excreting it is named Wilson's disease and in its later stages can be diagnosed by an eye examination, from the distinctive copper-colored rings-Kaiser-Fleischer rings- around the Iris of the eye. This can be successfully treated in a number of ways, drugs or Chelation, being the usual ones. Excess copper is known to be a causal factor and/or a potentiator of autism, Alzheimer's, bi-polar disorder, schizophrenia, Chronic Fatigue Syndrome (CFS) loss of mobility, hallucinations, low immune system function, loss of social function-the person becomes generally withdrawn-another autistic trait- liver disease, ADD, ADHD, ME (myalgic encephalomyelitis, a.k.a "yuppie flu") adrenal malfunction, depression, muscle withering and many more. It can trigger anorexia-the point is that CTS appears to be a psychological condition, whereas it's a physiological one- it takes a very good doctor to spot that. There is even a typical "Copper Toxicity Syndrome" personality, warm, caring, outgoing- very like Williams' sufferers.

    Basically if you suspect anyone in the family of having CTS, get a hair test, if the adult level is above 25 ppm (parts per million) see a specialist and change your lifestyle. For children, this is even more vital, as they can suffer permanent brain and Central Nervous System (CNS) damage. The CNS controls every function of the body. It is frightening how many CTS and Wilson's sufferers have and still do end up in psychiatric institutions because nobody did one standard test. Excess copper is a real threat to health! Tin-has been linked to some lung and eye conditions.

Fluoride: On the third of August 2012 Harvard University's School of Public Health published their findings of a study comprised of 27 research projects over a twenty-two year period, funded by The Federal National Institute for Health (NIH) on the effects of large (and it must be stressed, Large) concentrations of Fluoride in the public water supply on developing children. It concluded that virtually worldwide it significantly lowers IQ to a point of making already challenged children learning disabled (NLD), compared with children whose exposure to Fluoride was low or nil.

Lead (Chemical symbol Pb). Ironically it was copper which replaced Lead as the water piping of choice in the industrialized world. At one time it was used in paint and Pewter for plates and other household utensils, batteries, children's toys, fishing weights and cosmetics in some countries and it is still found everywhere in abandoned industrial sites. Its dangers cannot be overstated. Generally, lead mounts up in the body over years, either through the mouth, eyes, nose or skin.

The results, especially in children are both horrific and profound and can be fatal. They include a loss of memory, the full range of NLDs, mania/dementia, dramatic shifts of mood as well as more obviously physical symptoms, stomach pain, rashes and severe headaches. Treatment is effective if it's started quickly and is by Chelation therapy, the longer the delay in detecting and treating Lead poisoning the worse the permanent damage will be; this applies to any metal or other poison. During the eighteenth and nineteenth centuries-the hay-day of the traditional hat-making industry- Lead was used to stiffen, add weight and hold the shape of the hat Felt. The workers- who handled Lead all the time- became sick, which gave rise to the expression "as mad as a Hatter".

A quick mention of Iron (Chemical symbol Fe): Over-use of iron supplements or too much iron from another source causes damage to the liver, heart and brain. After the Iron is no longer being taken, recovery is usually pretty rapid with few if any complications in most instances. The exception is a rare genetic condition called Hemochromatosis when the liver stores Iron rather than regulating its level in the body by excreting any excess. Again it is treated with Chelation and perhaps dialysis, if the kidneys are damaged. With prompt treatment most people recover well.

Finally and perhaps the most dangerous of all, is Mercury(Chemical symbol Hg), also named "Quicksilver" on account of its color and that it is the only metal liquid at room temperature or in the sea, making exposure very easy, which only adds to its danger. It's highly destructive effects on the liver, kidneys, skin and brain have been well documented for decades. It can enter the body in numerous ways, oily fish such as Salmon and Tuna store Mercury from the sea, some from natural Mercury ores in the oceans, some from the appalling levels of Industrial dumping. The same applies to shellfish, especially clams and shrimp. It is in many clinical thermometers (although, due to the danger to patients- especially children- biting them, these are being phased out in favor of electronic versions) most barometers, light bulbs, some dyes, amalgam dental fillings, which have now been banned in most advanced countries like Germany since the early 1990's-to be replaced by safer, ceramic materials. I advise the replacement, if possible, of all dental amalgam fillings, a mix of Mercury, Silver, Tin and Copper to all my adult clients, not only to help safeguard against autism, but on general health grounds, as well. Mercury as vapor when heated can become airborne from industrial processes including mining and agricultural use and in hospitals, because like Copper it kills germs and fungi very efficiently. There are dozens of other sources too numerous to mention here. There is no longer any reasonable doubt at all that sufficient Mercury exposure can and does cause autism, most obviously ADHD by brain and immune system damage at any age. Further studies by America's renowned Harvard University, the CDC (Center for Disease Control) and the FDA (Food and Drug Administration) going back years confirm those findings.

If you believe there is any chance that you or your child could have become affected by metals, please go to a clinic and get tested today. There is also the much talked-about use of mercury compounds in common vaccines, most notoriously the MMR jab (Mumps, Measles and Rubella). It is used as Ethyl Mercury-named-Thimerosol as a vital preservative allowing the vaccine to "keep" for long periods, enabling it to be more widely available, especially for transportation to desperate countries in the Developing world.

Mercury has been used in scores of vaccines since the 1930's as it still is today, for example in HPV, Yellow Fever, Polio, Hepatitis B and Anthrax shots. Regrettably it is the best preservative we have to date -there is no viable alternative-clinically or financially.

If we want to keep helping mass populations around the world it is not only a clinical necessity but also a moral imperative.

The English Controversy:

In 1998 a team of researchers in London led by a Dr Andrew Wakefield published a report in The Lancet linking the MMR vaccine- and citing the Mercury in it as the cause-with gut problems and autism in babies given the jab. Shortly afterwards, having read the article written by Dr Wakefield, a number of the team disowned it as flawed, incompetent, faked, inadequately evidenced, unethical and unduly influenced by Wakefield's desire for financial gain. In fact only twelve carefully selected, already sick children had been hand-picked by Wakefield for his study and there were no proper comparative (Control) groups used to establish baseline results. That is, the expected norm, drawn from healthy children who had received the same vaccine and from a group of those who had not. Worse still, it emerged- slowly -that Wakefield's children had been seriously assaulted by being given painful, dangerous and completely un-necessary medical tests without proper parental consent. Parents had either not been informed at all or misinformed.

Despite numerous attempts by teams from around the world, Wakefield's results have never been repeated because they were a hoax and a lie from the outset. In 2004 The Sunday Times newspaper journalist Brian Deer investigated the whole squalid affair including Wakefield's dubious business dealings and associations, published his article and handed his files over to the British medical authorities in the shape of the General Medical Council (GMC) who then belatedly conducted their own investigation. Their report in 2010 completely discredited Wakefield and culminated with him being struck off the medical registers of both Britain and the US.

Meanwhile, the mistaken credibility that Wakefield had achieved by being published in the prestigious British medical journal The Lancet; caused worried parents to withdraw permission for their children to be vaccinated. Over the last fourteen years Britain and other countries, notably the USA have witnessed an ongoing and dramatic epidemic of Mumps, Measles and Rubella, causing some children to die and more to be permanently disabled.

Ten very good reasons to vaccinate yourself and your children:

1). Drug companies and their shareholders know that killing, maiming or poisoning their customers, children, pets, land or livestock is bad for business. That's why they spend Billions of Dollars (US) on the best laboratories, scientists and equipment available. To give one example: the best White Laser microscopes in the world are made by Siemens. AG- a personal opinion based on laboratory experience- and can cost upwards of five hundred thousand Dollars each. Their research costs are astronomical and the Patents last only fifteen years before some "bucket-shop lab" can copy the original formula and make a cheaper but vastly inferior product with untested low-grade ingredients. That is why big drug companies are forced to charge high prices; to finance future high quality research. In my opinion international drug patent law should change to twenty-five or thirty years, lowering costs and protecting the public.

2). Autism/AS along with associated gut conditions like Crohn's and Celiac disease existed well before the 1930's – or vaccines at all. Mercury-containing vaccines therefore can't logically be the cause.

3).Vaccination works: Polio vaccine for example cuts infection levels consistently by over eighty percent worldwide and reduces the severity of the illness for the minority who do still get it, even after vaccination. (Discover, January5th, 2012). The huge reward vastly outweighs the small risk involved.

4).Vaccination protects not only the vaccinated, but by cutting infection rates reduces disease even among the unvaccinated. This protects the whole community, reducing suffering and time lost at work or school while reducing the strain on local medical services. It is the socially responsible thing to do.

5).We vaccinate our pets, so why not our children and ourselves? Pet vaccine too contains the same trace Mercury preservatives- and I have yet to meet an autistic budgie or ferret.

6.) The Ethyl-Mercury compound, Thimerosol, having been in use since 1928 has, after the Wakefield furore been widely replaced in children's vaccines, although doing so has reduced their strength and shelf-life. It is still used for adult vaccinations. There has been no corresponding drop-off rate reported in Childhood Autism since and despite yet another WHO report confirming its safety, for whatever reason some people still refuse to vaccinate. The fact is the amount of mercury in a jab, compared with that from a lifetime of amalgam tooth fillings, eating sea foods or getting the actual purer form, Methyl- Mercury in your body by accident- is miniscule.

7). It is worth noting...children are given the MMR shot at eleven months- exactly the "crawling around putting things in their mouth stage-the discovery of the world outside themselves". If Mercury, or any other damaging contaminate enters them, vaccination is just about the least likely source. There may be an MMR booster shot given to a child at age four, but it isn't always needed and few concerns have ever been reported during the currently twenty-six years it has been in widespread use.

8). Not all vaccines even contain Mercury these days; the flu vaccine made by the Pasteur Institute in France is just one example. If you have concerns, ask for a Mercury-free product. Anyway, have the darn jab!

9).Talking of flu; you are far more likely to get Guillain-Barre Syndrome (a very rare and serious neurological condition) by having the flu than by having the jab-about, forty to seventy times more likely (WHO).

10). If the current take-up rate of common vaccinations about which we've known since their initial discovery by Edward Jenner in 1796 drops substantially, not only will the great plagues of the past such as Cholera and Diphtheria return, but there would be no money and therefore no research facilities left to develop new vaccines against current and future plagues, HIV being one. This would leave humanity open to possible catastrophe, as happened with The Black Death in the fourteenth century and who knows, maybe worse in the future? Each jab is an investment in your children's future, your grand children's future and that of the human race.

Random Fact on Vaccination: The first mass-vaccination program was conducted by Napoleon Bonaparte for his Grand Army in 1805, it was so successful that he ordered the program expanded to inoculate the whole of the French people in 1806 with such success that Bavaria and Hesse followed suit in 1807 and Denmark in 1810.

Advice for Jabs:

Yes; Jabs/Shots/Vaccinations, whichever is your preferred term do come with certain occasional risks of which we should be aware to take the necessary precautions, as should your Doctor. The younger or frailer the patient the greater is the risk although it is still tiny. Firstly; one person in a few hundred will suffer a marked reaction, such as a rash, soreness, redness/swelling where the shot was given or sleepiness, these need no treatment and will be fine in a few hours or days.

Occasionally the reaction can be a violent and perhaps even life threatening (why don't they call it "death-threatening"?) event, this allergic reaction is termed " anaphylactic shock" from some trace substance in the vaccine, as some unfortunate people get from common foods such as peanuts. The shock can be nearly instant or develop over five to ten minutes-which is why it is always wise to sit down for a while in the Doctor's surgery after a shot-just in case. In anaphylactic shock, the person goes into seizure and spasms, their air passages may swell up, causing choking and there may be cardiac arrest (heart stoppage). If this happens, the doctor will first administer epinephrine-a stimulant, using an "epipen", a spring-loaded syringe that delivers the shot immediately into a person's thigh muscle. He/she may then use CPR (cardio pulmonary resuscitation) to re-start the heart and lungs if needed or perhaps a defibrillator to deliver an electric shock to re-start the heart. Most patients recover very quickly and are fine. Patients with known serious allergies carry an epipen around with them at all times; my Father needed one for hornet stings. Secondly, especially for young children; check your child's temperature for fever for the five days before the vaccination appointment and on the day. The Doctor should do the same (and for adults as well) but not all do. If the person is sick-postpone.

Vaccinations DO put extra short-term strain on the immune system and if it's already fighting something else a jab can, in very rare instances "crash" it, with serious, perhaps long term consequences, including autism-if you are in any doubt, put off the appointment. For the same reason, take it easy for a few days after the jab, it should be making your immune system work harder to produce the antibodies to prevent the disease for which the vaccine was given. Afterwards: drink plenty of water get some extra rest and of course, you may feel mild symptoms of whatever you've been vaccinated against- that's normal. If you still feel off-color after four days, see a doctor.

Chelation:

In the previous section, "chelation" was used a lot in describing an effective way of treating heavy metal and toxic exposure, so here's how it works-and how it ties in with Autism. The word comes from the same Greek root as Chemistry and refers to the use of chemicals, in this therapy known as "Chelating agents" or

"Chelators" of which there are many, each one used according to the toxin it is intended to remove.

Chelation therapy goes way back to the Second World War where the first, named "British Anti Lewisite" (BAL) was invented in Oxford to combat the expected use by Germany of Lewisite-a spectacularly nasty Organo-arsenic gas-which in fact never existed. BAL did though prove an effective treatment for most heavy metals and poisonous minerals including Sulfur. It was discovered in 1940 but not declassified for public use until 1945. It is still used today, largely to treat Wilson's disease and Lead poisoning. BAL's chemical name is Dimercaprol.

Normally Chelators are put into the patient as a solution through a tube into a vein in the arm; this is the IV (Intravenous) method. Like most Chelators BAL has an oily feel to it. BAL though is injected by syringe, painfully, into large muscles. Chelators act by gluing themselves to the toxin, helping to break it up and making it slippery- that allows the body to move it away from regions of accumulation like the liver and into the body's normal systems until it can be excreted naturally via the kidneys-you drink lots of water-then basically remove the toxin through the urine. It requires lots of injections and has some nasty side effects.

Among those side effects: and this is true of any chelating agent is that it removes good things as well as bad, like vitamins and other nutrients, so supplementation is important during the treatment. BAL also causes vomiting, cramps, bone weakness, eye problems-it takes out the semi-fluid in the eye, causing (sometimes) blindness, - but most seriously it raises blood pressure very high, very quickly which can cause death from hemorrhaging in any major organ. Administered orally it tastes horrible, but is safer...but less effective. Other dangers include the risk of infection in the injection sites, Liver failure, and sudden (paradoxically) very low blood pressure causing unconsciousness (Blackouts) and like any substance there are the risks of a severe allergic reaction. These side effects and risks are far higher when the patient is a child.

As a result three better Chelators with fewer (but still significant) side effects were developed and are still widely used. One is DSMA, the second, EDTA and thirdly, DMPS-all very long sciencey names ☺. DMSA is the best for Lead. EDTA is used for most metals, which include the "soft" metal Calcium. All three can be taken by mouth but twenty to fifty, 2-4 hour IV sessions two or three times a week is the usual method of delivery for EDTA. The patient can walk around, watch Television or read while the IV is working. DMPS is used for Mercury; it is dangerous and not licensed by the FDA.

Orally, the treatment takes months, even years and is not as effective as by IV, really oral chelation works best as a prophylactic (prevention) action rather than a remedial one, compared with IV administration. That said, a high daily dosage of Vitamin C (2000+milligrams (mg) per day for an adult) and some other vitamins, minerals and herbs have shown promise as natural, gentle and effective Chelators of a number of toxins and metals.

Chelation and Autism:

There are doctors-and parents who believe both childhood and adult autism can be cured by "flushing the body" of toxic elements and indeed there have been some have well-reported success stories to tell from this approach. Please remember that these Chelators are powerful, unpleasant, dangerous chemicals in themselves, developed specifically for military and industrial emergency situations- and for ADULT USE, children have died or been horribly damaged by them.

With Chelation there is no way of predicting or controlling the results. For this reason, I have never suggested it, except when the patient, child or adult has direct blood-test or eye-witness proof of high metal/gas exposure-from whatever source. Whether the person is overtly autistic or not, should never be a part of that decision-making process. Nevertheless, as already mentioned, successes have happened, my guess is that the patient was made autistic by prior exposure; perhaps gradually over time before the treatment, in which case it would help, but only in a few cases and I repeat A FEW where the autism was caused by toxicity and there have not yet been sufficient high-quality clinical trials to put a figure on that "few". With any other of the causes we have discussed it would be a futile and dangerous risk. Furthermore, chelation is not a legally approved therapy for Autism in any major country to my knowledge, which, of course, does not stop its use by private or unlicensed so-called "clinics". Author's Note: Scarily, DMPS is actually available over-the-counter in some countries.

Case Study 2: Is there another use for adult chelation outside of emergencies?

The answer is: "Maybe", using EDTA to chelate calcium, magnesium and aluminum from the veins and arteries, gently for older people may help or prevent Parkinson's, Alzheimer's and those blockages which cause strokes and heart attacks because a lot of the plaques which cause the arterial hardening (not all) and brain damage are composed partly of those elements, in combination with some fats a.k.a. Lipids and some very specific types of protein. EDTA can act like a penetrating fluid, or kettle-descaler, which chemically-speaking, is pretty much what it is.

A Little experiment you can try at home ☺.

Take a glass, fill it with your normal drinking water, leave it 15 minutes, tip the water out and leave to dry. Check for residual scaling in the morning by holding it up to a light source, if it's cloudy-

that's likely to be calcium and magnesium just from the few drops left after tipping.

Author's question: Are hardened and blocked blood vessels more common among people whose water supply is high in calcium (and/or Magnesium) than those whose water is low in it? The answer, according to a 1996 study done in Glasgow, Scotland and Washington in 2002, as well as the opinion of America's world renowned Mayo clinic strongly suggest that it is. I advise those in "hard water" regions to drink distilled or filtered water. An expensive filter system or jug works well but is not essential; cheap, large filter papers bought from a chemist or general store do the same job effectively. Put the large cone-shaped paper inside a cheap plastic funnel; slowly pour the water through it into your normal glass and drink. Each paper can be dried, brushed clean and used quite a few times for economy.

Boiling water takes out a lot, but not all the impurities in it as well as killing any lurking germs in your supply. There is an assumption that well, river and bottled water, whether mineral or not is always safe. That is not necessarily true, all can contain high levels of minerals, metals and other elements, as well as bacterial or poison contamination. Fish do not climb out of the river to use the bathroom☺. In many regions ordinary tap (faucet) water can be the highest quality available.

In some countries EDTA is used legally to clear blocked coronary (Heart) arteries as a cheaper, effective, and less invasive option than open-heart surgery. It is certainly not a mainstream treatment (although it is used widely across the United States, Canada and in Japan), I am mentioning it, not promoting it, on the basis that it could-if it works-prevent some autism, heart attacks and dementia in the seniors age bracket which we have discussed. Once again, there is as yet insufficient clinical evidence to form a clear opinion.

Aspie Myth Busted: "Aspies and other Autists are deceitful and creepy because they avoid eye contact or stare at people". Well yes, we do avoid eye-contact, that is one of the diagnostic signs of autism and we do tend to look at people's right shoulders-so what? It doesn't make us creepy, rude or not listening- and it isn't an indication that we're not to be trusted.

Once again with these stupid myths the complete opposite is true. Autists are known to be more trusting, trustworthy, honorable, reliable and loyal than the average, because they lack normal social understandings. That naivety makes us far less likely to be successful con-artists, deceivers or manipulators. The apparent "staring" thing comes partly from the fact that Autists/Aspies blink less often than normal and can concentrate more intensely than NTs. Secondly one of the defining characteristics of Aspergers is an unsettlingly piercing gaze, something for which Sir Isaac Newton was noted and which some people find intimidating. That is not a valid excuse to discriminate against, or act with hostility towards anyone.

Chapter 6

The genetic roots of Classical Autism/ AS:

There are three purposes to this chapter, initially it is an introduction to the basics of how human genetics work in general and affect autism in all its forms in particular. It will then look at the most common expressions in the subject, unraveling some strange science terms along the way. It is not an attempt, by any means to explain fully, what is a massively complex bio-chemical field. Thirdly it is to prepare the ground for some original thoughts and theories in the following two chapters.

The first deals with Why autism may transfer from x parents to their children, yet not from y parents with a similar genetic make-up, to theirs. The succeeding chapter is a brand new causal theory for and explanation of, at least some cases of autism/AS and NLDs- of all types developing at any stage of life as the direct result of a bio-chemical chain of events, some of which we have already examined and some we have not and is hoped be of special interest to Veterans and their families everywhere. Autistic Factoid: Autistic/AS people often have one or more of the five senses (touch, smell, hearing, sight and taste) unusually well-developed. In my case it is hearing-I can hear dog-whistles and other higher pitches- but struggle more with the lower ends of the hearing scale.

By means of introduction to the practical genetics of autism, it is worth looking at the simplest inherited non-autistic condition which also very often goes hand-in-hand with autism as a co-morbidity; namely Factor-X Syndrome (FXS). William's Disease, as we know is caused by multiple gene "errors" on just one

Chromosome. Autism/AS are caused by a combination of multiple gene errors on several Chromosomes, making both very difficult to study. FXS on the other hand is caused by just a single error on a single gene named FMR1, on the X (Female) Chromosome. The X and Y pair of Chromosomes determine our gender, a baby with two X's becomes female, one with an X and a Y will be male. As such it is much easier to investigate than multiple gene/Chromosome conditions and by so doing scientists are able to learn much more about how genetics works in other situations, as its operating principles remain consistent throughout the whole human genome, with its staggering one billion combinations of "characters".

To help understand human genetics and the human genome itself, a good starting place is Matt Ridley's book, Genome (2000). This is widely regarded as an excellent and fun primer to the subject. He looks at various elements using each Chromosome to illustrate the chapter subject. It starts with the nature of DNA, explaining the four basic ACGT base pair chemical building blocks (Adenine, Cytosine, Guanine and Thymine) of human tissue. From combinations of any Three of these always e.g. AAC, every cell in us is built and placed according to its function. He then explores such diverse topics as the history of the subject: beginning with the nineteenth century monk Gregor Mendel who discovered the idea of "inheritance" by working with fruit flies through to the discovery of the purpose of DNA by Francis Crick and James Watson in Cambridge in 1953, which won both of them Nobel Prizes, on to the mechanics of how it works and to the first successful reading of the complete human genome in December 1999. This event was in itself the inspiration behind many books, including one by the project leaders, The Sanger Institute at Cambridge University sponsored by The Wellcome Foundation and led by the 2002 Nobel Prize winning biologist Prof Sir John Sulston and the Cold Spring Harbor Laboratory in New York State, USA, led by the same Prof James Watson, the co-discoverer of DNA. Along the way, Ridley guides us through some of the specialist areas of the subject, such as how genes are named and the functions of some of the more obscure ones, the Shank3 being a special example to which we shall return.

This shows plainly two vital things, firstly how complex the subject is "There are one billion words {characters} in the (Human instruction-Author's note) book {genome}... which makes it as long as 800 Bibles. If I read the genome out to you at the rate of one word per second, for eight hours a day, it would take a century" (Ridley, 2000). Secondly and perhaps even more excitingly for the researcher it illustrates how much more there is for us to learn-and how much opportunity there is for truly pioneering and world-shaking discoveries within the subject. Imagine the designs and images you could create from a one billion piece, four-color Lego ™ game set.

Currently we have read the full "instruction book" of the human genome, but have still to put it all in the correct order. We do not understand much about how one part affects the others and hence the overall function of the organism (human or otherwise). The genome, to some extent, resembles a quaternary machine code (a four character code, unlike, say, the computer base code which is binary, zero and one).

Many analogies have been drawn to illustrate its structure. One, to highlight the complexity of the task facing researchers was made concerning the corn genome by Professor Patrick Schnable. He is a Baker Professor of Agronomy and director of the Center for Plant Genomics and the Center for Carbon Capturing Crops, at Iowa State University. Schnable likened it to a jigsaw puzzle.

It is a big jigsaw and it takes immense computer power and time to assemble the final picture correctly. Due to its huge size, the task of scanning and compiling the entire human code has been broken down into designated genomic "territories" each of which is being sequenced and finished by different University teams (and some private companies) around the world. The findings of these teams constantly provide both the latest knowledge and the interpretations of its meaning; bearing in mind new discoveries are being made literally on a daily basis. Because this book is in part about the genetics that affect autism, it is mainly the teams working on those relevant chromosomes that we'll be looking at.

The first is based at Stanford University, Palo Alto, California, a pivotal member of which is Dr Donna Spiker. In a 1999 lecture, Dr Spiker, Clinical Director of the Stanford University Autism Research Program, speaking about the families of Fragile X Syndrome sufferers, explained "They have a risk 50-75 times greater than the general population. These families may exhibit a genetic form of autism. That is, to pass along autism through their genes".

Alongside her perfect definition of genetic inheritance, she makes a vital point about autism, Fragile X is not strictly an autistic disorder, but in an astonishingly high sixteen percent of cases, the sufferer is severely or profoundly autistic as well. To emphasize the significance of that 16%, we are reminded that the average incidence of autism in the general population is, according to the American Society of Autism (ASA) only that 1-2%. From Dr Spiker we learn that classical autism can be inherited as a side effect or vector from other different heritable conditions and not just by a complex but by a specific Chromosomic recoding as it is with Asperger's Syndrome. This reveals both the full scope of the issue and again fully highlights its relevance, not just for those teaching or caring for single-syndrome autistics, but for multi-syndrome ones as well and some non-autistic people like Fragile X patients. FXS children are always physically (often severely) disabled, have ADHD, elongated ears and faces, mental incapacity, reproductive deformities, very high anxiety levels (which is also true of all autistic/AS people) aggression, foot problems, shyness (like Aspies), heart problems and epilepsy-and that like Autism, boys are far more likely to inherit it than girls-we don't know why, perhaps Prof Baron-Cohen's theory of fetal testosterone exposure is behind that statistic?

The next major group to look at is the archives of the Online Mendelian Inheritance in Man project, named after Gregor Mendel (OMIM, 2005). These are the internet published findings of the team working at the Johns Hopkins University in Maryland, spearheaded by Dr Victor McKusick. It is a vast database of all known human genes, together with their reference mark on the genome and with full clinical and experimental descriptions of what they are known to do. OMIM is a close collaborator with Medline. Medline/ PubMed is a highly popular and very reputable website covering every facet of medicine and is well worth checking out.

All types of Classical Autism are caused by a number of code errors on more than one gene/Chromosome which cumulatively cause enough damage to be recognizable as autism, or, of course any other inherited trait, like eye color. To take a topical example: to confirm the discovery of the remains of King Richard III of England in February 2013 the Leicester University archeological team responsible for the find needed to compare the DNA of the remains with that of a known living relative. The relative who confirmed the germ line was a Canadian gentleman named Michael Ibsen, a direct descendant of Richard's eldest sister, Anne of York.

When the King's face was finally reconstructed, the resemblance, even after five centuries of generations between him and Mr. Ibsen was simply breath-taking and shows the awesome power of genes. Our genes give us our most basic form as individuals, our "Hard-wiring", our inheritance. We are largely the product of them. This tells us a lot about autism as a condition. If we can inherit features, we inherit conditions and tendencies. Nothing is in isolation; the combinations of code which make classical autism make the person different in other ways too, not only by "ordering" a different brain structure but by changing the whole puzzle picture. That is what makes Autism a "Whole Body Condition", because it affects not only the brain, but many other of the physical functions as well. This is one example gene, which forms part of that equation. AUTS4 is found at 15q11-13q (Chromosome 15) on the genome.

Author's note: I'm looking to keep these arcane names to a minimum except where they serve a strong purpose. They are best regarded as a type of three-dimensional map reference, which pinpoints the physical position of each gene within the double helix genome structure, as shown in the illustration sections of this book.

That same gene also predisposes people to Glaucoma, Large Cell Lymphoma and significantly for this book, Celiac disease, among many. The issue of "predisposition or "susceptibility" here is important. Having a certain gene does not always mean the person will have the related condition, those cases are known as "dormancy." It does mean, as do incidences of non-inherited "spontaneous mutation" that they ("they" are "carriers") can pass it on to subsequent generations or "down through the germ line," who may suffer from it.

Returning to the issue of the Shank3 gene, found on Chromosome 22-q3. This work introduces another team, that of Professor Thomas Bourgeron at the famous Pasteur Institute in Paris, France. Bourgeron believes autism to be a neurosynaptic condition and discovered that many autistic people and especially those with Asperger's Syndrome have a double copy of that gene's sequence. Brain imaging has proved that those people's brain synapses are structurally different from the average in the regions which deal with certain social and cognitive tasks. This makes Shank3 an excellent causal candidate for some aspects of autism. If and until larger studies can verify Bourgeron's findings, we can't be sure, as a majority of our genes are involved with, to a greater or lesser degree, the development of our brain.

Other teams working at Cambridge, Newcastle and Cardiff in the UK have noted sequence abnormalities consistent with autism on Chromosomes 2, 3, 6, 12 and 15. The most likely scenario is that enough abnormality causes autism and the places where it occurs may determine the specific condition, for example, Dyslexia. Dr Fred Volkmar, Head of Child Medicine at Yale University and one of the world's leading specialists in Autism, believes that up to six major genes and as many as thirty minor ones may be involved scattered across several Chromosomes with each playing a role (Nature Genetics, 2007).

Summary: Briefly we inherit twenty three sets of Chromosomes from each parent, making 23 pairs. Each Chromosome contains of a number of genes, a few hundred in some, a few thousand in others. All in all a person has a little over 20, 000 genes. All of these are known collectively as "The human Genome" and are contained in our RNA and DNA. DNA is the program (code) which, via RNA, a kind of chemical messenger, tells each cell what to be and where to go to assemble a complete human being, mouse, tree or whatever, like assembling a giant jigsaw puzzle, as Dr Schnable says.

Each gene and each sequence (Line) of genes does something different, or nothing, if they remain switched off, which a lot do. The genes that are switched on are said to be "Expressed" to make them build their assigned piece of the body at a pre-determined time during development, after all there would be no point in building a leg before the heart or brain. If at any point the code is faulty or becomes corrupted, by, for example radiation, programming errors will occur and these are the genetic diseases and weaknesses which are often in the news. The same principle applies with our jigsaw puzzle parallel, if some of the pieces are wrong, or put in the wrong places; the picture on the board will be different from the one on the box.

The genome-and this is really important to know- is active throughout the whole of life, from the moment of conception onwards and can be affected by genes being switched on or off at any time (changing the body and mind) by various factors including the toxins we have discussed and the therapies we will discuss later. It is not only negative influences which can trigger conditions, so too can positive ones-the birth of a child, winning a big career promotion or gaining fame, by the same mechanism-things change, for good or bad, sometimes in profound ways.

Genetic and Autie Factoids: There is even a gene which determines whether our earwax is hard or soft, it's called ABCCII discovered by scientists at Nagasaki University in Japan in 2006. Autists by observational and medical research have been shown to produce more earwax than NTs and need to have their ears checked-and flushed regularly-the recommendation is every three months. Excess or impacted earwax can cause loss of balance, which may be mis-interpreted as "clumsiness", as well as hearing difficulty, which will interfere with education and general communication.

It has also long been observed by some specialists that autistics seem more likely to be borderline or actually anemic (a lack of red blood cells) causing tiredness and general malaise which may be easily misdiagnosed as "depression" or "malingering". It's another example of the Whole Body Condition.

Human DNA - The Double Helix

Chapter 7

OCD, electric lights and a cat named Smike:

Genetic expression can be influenced at any time by physical and emotional, as well as toxic circumstances-if the relevant genetic sequence for that change is in your individual genome already- or occurs by spontaneous mutation. Throughout the ages there have been rare but well-documented and photographed instances of people whose hair has turned white overnight after a traumatic experience such as the death of a sibling, spouse, an accident or loss of a long- cherished family pet, or career. The shock switches on all the genes for gray hair at once rather than over a period of years as normally happens, it happened to Shah Jehan, builder of the Taj Mahal in Agra, India on hearing of the death of his wife, Muntez. Exactly the same applies when someone's hair drops out overnight. Cancer can be triggered by shock. All those people had the sequences for greyness or baldness already, otherwise it could not have happened, they just needed "the trigger", and the same precept is equally true of dozens of other conditions.

OCD-Obsessional Compulsive Disorder:

It can be a ritualized form of stammer, facial or other tic and Tourette's. It is, as we saw from the DSM IV and ICD particularly likely to affect autistic and AS people because of their psychological trait of searching for security within fixed routines-which is fine -up to a certain point. It is manifested by the extreme, sometimes life disrupting expressions in the stereotyped and constant repetition of behaviors, patterns of thought or mannerisms referred to in those books, as well as to the compulsive sticking to pointless and even self-defeating routines and tasks. They do things in a set order, being obsessive about the placement of objects on a shelf or in a room and many more compulsive acts, such as hoarding newspapers or cleaning dishes up to two hundred times a day are common examples; in other words actions that make a person virtually a recluse from society and destroys their lives.

Clearly such a person is unlikely to find employment or companionship among other things. OCD has anxiety as its wellspring, another very autistic trait, as we know. When OCD presents in someone who has already been diagnosed as autistic, doctors call it Obsessive Compulsive Personality Disorder (OCPD) to distinguish it from those exact same symptoms in non-Autists. OCPD is an accepted member of the Autism Family. "The roots of compulsive behavior are to be found in the experience of fear or trauma" (Hale).

OCD's manifestations in non- autistic people are mainly superstitions, like wearing a lucky charm, not walking under ladders, touching someone with curly hair and some of the rituals top sports players do whilst playing. A good example is how the Great Russian tennis champion, Maria Sharapova carefully avoids walking on the lines between points and games, the Spanish legend, Rafa Nadal too, has elaborate rituals on court. Cricketers' rituals make an outstanding study of OCD as well☺. There are two important things to note about these. Firstly, they enhance and not destroy the person's performance and focus and secondly they are perfectly innocent and are no-one's business. There is nothing wrong with any healthy routine which works for you; these things only become an issue at the point where they make normal life hard or impossible for yourself or others. Interestingly, studies have shown that people with OCD tend to be, while socially dysfunctional, very meticulous, very good at detail, very determined and of above average intelligence-just like HFAs, and Schizophrenics, can there be possible genetic links?

However, severe OCDs are beatable. I know because I had one. Let's be very honest, an OCD is a form of addiction, pure and simple, the result of performing the compulsive acts-whatever they are-is the relief of anxiety and an accompanying euphoric pleasure caused by the release of chemicals in the brain called endorphins- the natural "highs"/"uppers". People who work-out hard or run get that same high, for the same reason, it is very addictive and as a result very tough to beat.

Case Study 3: My compulsion was the switching on and off of electric light switches of any kind, mainly clandestinely at home. I would wait until my parents were asleep, and then tiptoe barefoot around the house, checking every switch and flicking them on and off up to a hundred or more times each including the outside ones; which were horrible, especially during the cold, wet, windy English winters. This started at the age of eleven, when we moved from a single level bungalow into a two storey house and continued until the age of about twenty five or six when some people at work spotted the same behavior there. The first few times I laughed it off, then after a couple more times realized that it was potentially a career-breaker, colleagues were beginning to talk to me about it and asking if I had a problem, or wanted to speak to a counselor: Which I didn't, I felt ashamed and was afraid it would go against my career record and damage my future prospects-a not uncommon thing, as I have learned from countless clients since-plus counselors are usually expensive. The worst thing was that I had no control over it because I had no idea why I was doing it, just that without it, I couldn't sleep-a common problem for Autists of all types for many reasons. Folklore: Some have found that simply by moving their bed round to face North (Head-end- South greatly improves their sleep, feng shui or what :-).

    I read up on the subject from some books recommended by my boss-a wonderful lady who happened to be the senior psychology lecturer-I was teaching in a college at the time... They gave me the first and most important steps to beating OCD or any other addiction-the understanding and acceptance that I had a real problem secondly that other people had it too, and thirdly that I had a very strong motive to overcome it. So I thought and thought about it-over months and at the same time tried to fight it-which didn't really work- it just made me very irritable, stressed and shaky although I did force myself to semi-stop at work, but increased the behavior outside-so even more people thought I was "strange" (ha-ha).Then one day-during a coffee break, I suddenly remembered the key to it all in a sort of flashback. I was asleep at home aged five or six and only recently back from hospital after having my appendix out-which in itself was traumatic. I woke up to foul-smelling smoke and flames and sparks coming from the bedroom light switch-which was too high for me to reach. I ran into my parents' bedroom and woke them up-still in pain from the recently-removed stitches and my Dad came in, opened the window, switched the house electricity off, put the fire out and then tied off and wrapped insulation tape round all the wiring as I knelt on the end of the bed and watched. In the morning he showed me what had happened. It was a cheap brown plastic switch fitment, with frayed, cotton-coated old-fashioned brown wiring, which had shorted out and caught fire, set the switch alight, which then melted the plastic. The house was only seven years old but had been poorly built by a drunken sub-standard builder.

When our family moved into the two storey house my subconscious must have recalled the event and thought, "suppose it happens again, downstairs in the night and we are all asleep upstairs, you will all burn to death". At that moment I was cured. I had seen the face of the fear and realized that in modern, properly inspected buildings, at home or at work, it just wasn't going to happen again. I have never done such behavior or had any other OCD symptom since, nor anything similar. That sense, during the coffee break of discarding the shackles of two decades made me cry.

I was lucky that the combination of reading, self-analysis and the support of professional colleagues created that coffee-break insight and epiphany. For people without such support, counseling of various types, whether one-to-one analysis with a professional psychologist, group therapy or Cognitive Behavioral Therapy (CBT) can be equally useful. If not then I recommend a skilled and certified hypnotist who by "regressing" the mind down the memory of the years can find the event(s) which lie at the core of a person's psyche and, by exposing it, make it fight-able. That process is called "running the trauma", I have seen several live, successful demonstrations of its usefulness, as well as doing it myself with patients many times.

There are also prescribed Psycho-active (those which affect the brain) medications which can alleviate the symptoms of OCD, the most likely to be prescribed is a Selective Serotonin Re-uptake inhibitor (SSRI) such as Celexa, Paxil or Prozac. These drugs act to both stabilize mood swings and as antidepressants; they are "chill-out" drugs and can be very beneficial and life-empowering for some people, yet non-effective or damaging to others. The drugs act by fooling the brain into thinking it has more Serotonin (the happy brain chemical) than it does, making it act that way. The prevailing theory (and it is only that, not a proven fact yet) is that low Serotonin levels are the cause of clinical depression, which can trigger anxiety and hence OCD. However, like most drugs they can have side-effects, including loss of self-motivation, self-esteem, lethargy, nausea, a well-documented increased risk of suicide, rashes (sometimes) and loss of sex drive (Libido). On top of those, they tend to be addictive and can cause long term liver damage. I feel, as with Ritalin for ADD that they should be used only (if at all) as a treatment of last resort in the most challenging of cases and under the strictest supervision. The second preferred types of drug to relieve all types of anxiety (Antiaxiolytics) are the Benzodiazepines; the most popular and best of which, in my opinion is Xanax made by the Pfizer Company of Brooklyn, New York.

Appropriate instances for this drug treatment are people who find they either unwilling or unable to talk about their experiences because it makes them feel worse and each session only "restimulates the original trauma" to unbearable levels. It is a normal and not terribly uncommon situation. For some hypnosis may not be possible or do more harm than good by re-stimulation or if someone's memory has become so deeply buried in the subconscious that it is unreachable.

Case Study 4: Smike was a tiny, black, rain- soaked, starving kitten, a few weeks old, who my parents found in a gutter one evening and adopted, years before I was born. They wrapped him in a small blanket, fed him and put him in a little basket near the fireside. Over time, with love and care he got better and bigger and they called him "Smike" after the poor boy who Nicholas befriended in Charles Dickens' novel, Nicholas Nickleby

For a year or two afterwards, every time they did cleaning, moved furniture and sometimes outside, they found little caches of food that Smike had hidden away from the memories of his bad times and treatment. Later on, fully settled and content, that stopped, showing how compulsive, anxiety-driven repetitive behavior can sometimes be overcome by kindness and trust, no matter how early or deep the original trauma. Smike lived on happily until the age of fifteen and a half.

Chapter 8

PTSD and Autism, is there a link?

Post-Traumatic Stress Disorder, sometimes referred to as "shell shock" "survivor's guilt" or "battle fatigue", among other things, can be caused by a single physical or emotional event such as 9/11, a violent assault, a motor accident or a series of events over a long period, abuse and childhood bullying being the two most powerful sources; horror of any nature or impossible family circumstances- like caring for and watching a loved one decline and die- and that can include an animal companion. When its cause is cumulative-by the slow-erosion of emotional reserves-some psychologists term it Complex-PTSD, (C-PTSD). In either situation, both the ICD and DSM IV are more-or-less in agreement on its telltale signs and symptoms. It can be likened to a battery being drained, leaving the person uncomfortably numbed-out and lacking "spark" and any enjoyment of life.

There is nothing new about PTSD; the modern definitions below have been recorded down the ages by contempories, historians, observers and ordinary citizens in people who have survived earthquakes, volcanoes, floods and other natural disasters, as well as soldiers and sailors returned from war. PTSD is normal; it is not a sign of weakness. Weakness is when a person denies it and does not seek help; the truly strong confront it and do something- that is courage, the acceptance of one's humanity.

The DSM IV criteria for PTSD are:

A. The person has been exposed to a traumatic event in which both of the following have been present:

(1)The person experienced, witnessed, or was confronted with an event or events that involved actual or threatened death or serious injury, or a threat to the physical integrity of self or others

(2) The person's response involved intense fear, helplessness, or horror. Note: n children, this may be expressed instead by disorganized or agitated behavior: Author's note-perhaps ADHD?

B. The traumatic event is persistently re-experienced in one (or more) of the following ways:

1) Recurrent and intrusive distressing recollections of the event, including images, thoughts, or perceptions. Note: in young children, repetitive play may occur in which themes or aspects of the trauma are expressed: Author's note, another strongly Autistic trait, the evidence mounts.

2) Recurrent distressing dreams of the event. Note: In children, there may be frightening dreams without recognizable content sometimes called "Night terrors", which may also been caused by an undiagnosed physical illness, fast, professional help is vital in either situation.

(3) Acting or feeling as if the traumatic event were recurring (includes a sense of reliving the experience, illusions, hallucinations,

and dissociative flashback episodes, including those that occur upon awakening or when intoxicated).Note: in young children, trauma-specific reenactment may occur. (They re-live the experience)-Hale.

(4) Intense psychological distress at exposure to internal or external cues that symbolize or resemble an aspect of the traumatic event.

(5) Physiological reactivity on exposure to internal or external cues that symbolize or resemble an aspect of the traumatic event.

C Persistent avoidance of stimuli associated with the trauma and numbing of general responsiveness (not present before the trauma), as indicated by three (or more) of the following:

Efforts to avoid thoughts, feelings, or conversations associated with the trauma
Inability to recall an important aspect of the trauma
Efforts to avoid activities, places, or people that arouse recollections of the trauma

(4) Markedly diminished interest or participation in significant activities

Feeling of detachment or estrangement from others

Restricted range of affect (e.g., unable to have loving feelings

A sense of a foreshortened future (e.g., does not expect to have a career, marriage, children, or a normal life span)

D. Persistent symptoms of increased arousal (not present before the trauma), as indicated by two (or more) of the following:

(1) Difficulty falling or staying asleep

(2) irritability or outbursts of anger

(3) difficulty concentrating

(4) hyper-vigilance (always "keyed up and can't relax or "let their guard down" –author's note).

(5) Exaggerated startle response

Author's note: This "startle response" is a prime indicator of the condition; you get the patient to chat, relax, have a cup of tea and ask an assistant, un-noticed to tap them lightly on the shoulder, or make a sharp noise. If the person "jumps" obviously, then PTSD is basically confirmed.

E. Duration of the disturbance (symptoms in Criteria B, C, and D) is more than one month.

F. The disturbance causes clinically significant distress or impairment in social, occupational, or other important areas of functioning.

The ICD (v 10) section F43. 1 says almost exactly the same things; there is no need to repeat them. The important thing to bear in mind is that the patient was perfectly healthy before the event(s) which triggered their condition. There are two answers to the question of whether there is a link between PTSD and Autism, one of them is a near- definite "yes" and the second, in this author's experience is also "yes".

Firstly, a team at Boston University supported by the American VA (Veteran's Affairs, who, despite poor funding, attempts to care for ex-service people) and led by Dr Mark Miller, a specialist clinical psychologist. Dr Miller studied the genomes of hundreds of traumatized Veterans and other volunteers before publishing a preliminary report in "VA Research Currents" online magazine in August, 2012. He found a statistically significant number of his PTSD patients compared with the healthy volunteers carried one particular sub-type of the RORA gene, which expresses in the brain and affects our emotional states and responses, among other things. This and many other sub-types of RORA figure prominently in the genomes of Autists, especially HFAs, and Aspies, making RORA another prime candidate for being one of the "autistic genes", as predicted by Drs Volkmar and Bourgeron and further supported by the research of Dr Christopher Badcock, of the London School of Economics (LSE) one of Britain's top Universities, as he explained in his book, "The imprinted Brain".

This gives us a firmer indication as to why some people are more likely than others to suffer PTSD in any given situation and also why two people may suffer the same traumatic experience with one going on to develop PTSD, while the other does not. It could also explain why autistic people are more likely than NTs to experience PTSD and why many of the PTSD symptoms, the increased risk of suicide being one, match those of Autism/AS, notably being emotionally "closed in" and ADHD. These conditions appear to derive from the same or similar specific genetic profiles. From this I believe derives the second "yes", linking PTSD to Autism- that traumatic experiences can cause autism, as well as its other noted effects to develop at any age by activating previously dormant genes already in certain people to suddenly express, causing autism to present. This process could be caused by a variety of stressors; Toxins or life-changing experiences whether they are negative like trauma, or positive, like a huge lottery win.

These same changes can also occur due to a second genetic process at work, namely Epigenetics. Epigenetic change is not the changing of the DNA sequencing itself from within, but changes and mutations outside the DNA by things like toxic exposures etc., etc. as with Autism, which affect it and therefore physical and mental health, via gene "expression" that cannot be passed on through the generations. PTSD can be caused by this process-and who knows, maybe more.

The influential nineteenth century German philosopher Freidrich Nietzsche wrote "that which doesn't kill us, makes us stronger", he should have added "or gives us PTSD and perhaps our offspring, Depression and/or Autism as well". Again, we must stress the universal lesson that genetics seek to teach us, that there is no blame, no weakness, no shame and no stigma to these things, just a combination of biophysics, a "trigger" and "susceptibility". One thing affects everything, big and small, good and bad. "From this understanding emerges tolerance and compassion, from these we should kindle the fires of progress" (Hale). Further evidence for this process comes from the fact that stress has well proven links to cancer; heart attacks and to triggering Shingles in people who carry the Chickenpox virus, all by damaging their immune systems. These are all purely physical manifestations. I submit that by the same argument, trauma can trigger autism, because it has clear physical causes lying deep within the human brain, by that self-same mechanism PTSD also has clear physical causes and manifestations within the brain, including, as has already been medically established, TBIs.

Professor Tian Xu, a geneticist at Yale University said: "A lot of different conditions can trigger stress signaling - physical stress, emotional stress, infections, inflammation – all these things.

Reducing stress or avoiding stress conditions is always good advice" (The Daily Telegraph, Jan 14h, 2010). The most convincing evidence, proving that in children at least, mental and/or emotional abuse and neglect alone actually physically changes the structure of the brain to produce PTSD-like effects was conducted by the McMaster University of Ontario in Canada and was revealed by its co-author, the notable psychiatrist Dr Harriet MacMillan in the July 30th edition of the US News & World Report, 2012. She wrote "The main message for child health clinicians and people working with children is that psychological maltreatment is just as harmful as other types of maltreatment".

"We know that exposure to other types of maltreatment like physical and sexual abuse can be associated with a broad range of types of impairment in physical and mental health, and cognitive and social development," she said. "Similarly, we see these types of impairments associated with psychological maltreatment." The same is true of emotional abuse or the with-holding of unconditional love and of course bullying, all these affect the body as well as the mind. A Savant 3: The strange experience of surgeon Dr Anthony Cicoria, born in 1952 and now Chief of the Medical Staff and Chief of

Orthopedics at Chenango Memorial Hospital, Norwich, New York. Dr Cicoria was struck by lightning in 1994 while standing next to an outdoor telephone booth. He was badly burned and his heart stopped-he needed resuscitation-luckily a trained nurse was standing just behind him. He was taken to hospital and quickly released, although he was feeling energy- drained and had difficulty in remembering things, so he saw a neurologist, who could find nothing wrong. A few weeks later Dr Cicoria began to develop an interest in playing and listening to the piano to a near obsessive degree.

    He bought one and taught himself to both play and compose within three months of his accident, he noted that his head seemed full of music, to which he devoted every spare moment. A very successful parallel career as a pianist/composer began in Vermont in 2007, his skills and fame continue to grow; he has produced many CD's and can be appreciated on YouTube ™. Until being electrocuted, the Doctor had shown no noticeable interest in or talent for music. A similar incident occurred in August 1800 to a slow and sickly baby born in the small coastal town of Lyme Regis, Dorset, England. The child's name was Mary Anning, who from that moment became strong and clever; she went on to become famous as the "Mother of modern Paleontology"-the greatest and most successful fossil-hunter and recordist who has ever lived.

Chapter 9

The left-handed Connection:

It has long been known that left-handed people are more likely to be Dyslexic than their right-handed counterparts. Left-handedness, is like classical autism genetically passed, so in left-handed families with Dyslexia in the genes the probability of any family member being Dyslexic and left -handed is much higher than the statistical average. Around 10% of the global population are left-handed (The Week, April 27th, 2012) they are more likely to be schizophrenic than the general population, but also more likely to have genius-level IQ s and/or be more artistic than right-handers. Examples include Albert Einstein, Michelangelo, Leonardo Da Vinci, Bill Gates, Bill Clinton, Sir Isaac Newton, Benjamin Franklin, and

Aristotle, guitarist Jimi Hendrix, Vincent Van Gogh, Marvin Hagler (Boxer) Thomas Jefferson, H G Wells, Alexander the Great, Ringo Starr, Marie Curie, Martina Navratilova, Barack Obama Mahatma Gandhi, Angelina Jolie, Thomas Jefferson (to whom I am blood related) and Charles Darwin. Left-handedness is slightly less common in women than men. Lefties are more prone to addictions- principally alcohol. Jack the Ripper was left-handed, as was The Boston Strangler and the gangster, John Dillinger.

Left-handedness also runs strongly through the British Royal Family, Queen Victoria, King George VI, The Queen Mother, Queen Elizabeth II, Prince Charles and his son Prince William were/are all left-handers. To illustrate the lefty/Autist connection, in a 1983 study by Prof Lars C Gillberg a leading child psychiatrist from the University of Gothenburg in Sweden, among autistic/AS children and in comparison with a peer group of non-autistic ones, found around 15% of left-handedness among non-autistics, of the others a staggeringly high 37% were left-handed/ambidextrous, that is, use both hands equally, but are not right-hand dominant. Similar results have been broadly replicated since by other teams, indicating in the clearest possible way that there is a firm genetic link between left-handedness and autism. Why should this be?

My own research has suggested one possible reason at least. The brain is actually two brains, the left and right hemispheres which are connected by a tissue/nerve bridge called the Corpus Collasum. In right-handed people, the left side of the brain is dominant, in lefties, the right dominates. In cases of autism in general and AS in particular, where the structure of the left side of the brain is more commonly inherently different from standard, or in non-classical instances, damaged, left-handedness would make sense. In my case, I throw right and catch left, play cricket right, but table tennis and badminton left, Pool-either way is fine. Nirvana's founder and guitarist, Kurt Cobain, played left, but wrote (usually) right as does the Spanish tennis star, Rafael Nadal. Exactly the same applies to hearing and sight and to football; Auties/AS tend to be left ear, eye and foot dominant, as compared with NTs.

We must logically conclude that there is a connection between dyslexia, Autism and the left-handed tendency. This again brings us back to the tricky debate about whether Dyslexia (and for that matter, Dyscalculia) are members of the Autism or NLD families. It is my opinion-and it is no more than that, based on observation- that they can be either, as not all dyslexics are autistic by any means, but quite a few autistics/AS are dyslexic. The question has as yet no definitive answer; it works on a person-by-person basis, it is one of the many contradictions in the study of Autism which science has yet to resolve and which this book deliberately does not shrink from recognizing.

Author's note: Please, never ever try to "turn" a naturally left-handed child to conform with right-handed society, no matter how good the intention. Doing so will cause neurological confusion, resulting in many potential disorders including poor co-ordination, anxiety, compulsive, sometimes self-destructive habits, depression, dyslexia and lack of muscle memory. These conditions will tend to exaggerate as the child approaches adulthood and continue doing so throughout it, to a point where very serious mental consequences may occur.

The correct thing is to encourage and re-assure the child about left-handedness and make sure that the school and staff have the materials and knowledge that is needed. If they don't, make a fuss and make/buy/adapt as much equipment at home as possible, for example something as simple as whittling down hexagonal pencils or crayons to being duel-sided for easier grip. Cricket bat bases are also very easy to chamfer down to left-leaning.

Chapter 10

Boys and Girls:

Hemophilia is sometimes known as "the bleeding disease" because the sufferer lacks some, or all of the chemical which makes blood clot, in the past before modern treatments, it was life-threatening, as the slightest cut, knock or bruise to the body or head could result in death. It is also nicknamed "The Royal disease"- Queen Victoria was a carrier and her daughters spread it into almost every Royal House of Europe, most notably Portugal and Russia. The Russian Empress, Alexandra, wife of Tsar Nicholas II was a carrier and their heir, Alexis was a severe hemophiliac-the only person who seemed able to treat him-and who saved his life many times was the notorious monk, Rasputin.

As a result, his influence at court grew and grew leading to jealousy from the nobility he had supplanted and horror from the Russian people because of his reportedly debauched lifestyle and rumors of an affair with Alexandra. Rasputin was murdered by a cadre of nobles in 1916. A year later the people rebelled in the Russian Revolution which first removed and then murdered the Tsar and his whole family. It's one of those interesting historical "what ifs". If Alexis had not been a hemophiliac, there would have been no Rasputin at court-and perhaps no revolution.

Hemophilia is purely a genetic condition affecting only males, because its genetic code is carried on the female X chromosome. Such single-gender conditions are unusual and called "Autosomal Dominant" For most conditions the child has to inherit a copy of the condition's gene from each parent-those are "autosomal Recessive" cases. We have seen earlier that there are genetic conditions which affect only females and others which affect the genders unequally, that is, have a strong gender bias, Autism and AS are two such.

Well confirmed research by Dr Tony Attwood (1998) and Prof Gillberg among many, suggested the ratio for AS is just above 4:1, (Male) other studies have varied that figure to some extent, however the central point that autism and AS are way more common in males than females remains clear, with some showing the ratio as high as 15:1. What is also clear though and I have found this, is than when females have AS they have it far more severely than males, the same is true of dyslexia, again indicating that some forms of dyslexia are certainly autistic in origin. The reasons are not as yet fully explainable.

As diagnosis has improved, as it has since the early 1990's one might have expected to see that ratio drop for a number of reasons. In many societies female education was-and in some, still is- regarded as unimportant and girls had little or no schooling and hence little chance of being formally diagnosed, as the male was expected to be the breadwinner. Secondly, some symptoms of AS, in particular the avoidance of eye contact would be regarded as "proper, even desirable female behavior", as would the quiet, home and peace-loving nature of Autists and Aspies and again gone undiagnosed. Additionally girls tend to be less physically aggressive in communicating their emotions and are, compared with boys, less likely to attract the kind of attention that may lead to a psychiatric assessment and even if they do, it is all too often put down to "hysteria "or "hormones" and ignored . One further factor is that in many cultures parents were/ are far less likely to send daughters to psychiatrists for fear of stigmatizing the family and reducing the chances of advantageous marriages for both genders. Yet, as these attitudes have changed and diagnosis has become more available and accurate the ratio has, if anything increased, again adding extra weight to Prof Baron-Cohen's theories.

Autism fact: "Rain Man": The 1988 movie by Barry Levinson was based closely on a real, badly brain damaged boy who became a legend, Kim Peek. He remembered every word, date and time of anything he ever read. He could be given a random date, say 12/9/70 and immediately say what day of the week it was (a Saturday) for instance, the same with addresses and telephone numbers or car plates, just staggering.

Chapter 11

The Importance of early diagnosis: Dr Phillip Kendall of the Temple University, Philadelphia wrote in 2001... "Without {early} treatment the prognosis for persons with autistic disorders is not guarded…..nor do they develop the ability to interact socially in ways that are considered normal". This clearly applies to the classroom situation too. His point is further reinforced in context by Simon Franke "…it is increasingly important to develop more effective early teaching interventions…and (popular) strategies" (In Touch, 2007 King's College London Journal- pp12-14).

To succeed fully for each individual, diagnosis must be early and the study of genetics can help achieve this goal. Toward this end, the teacher and scientist should work together hand-in-hand. The design of this book mirrors the structure of that vital partnership deliberately, in order to highlight it. Kate Wall in her 2004 Autism and Early Years Practice asserts, "The importance of practitioner {Teacher} awareness and understanding of Autistic Spectrum Disorders is once again highlighted as a fundamental element of effective assessment and provision" That statement was an inspiration for this project's attempt to aid both awareness and diagnostics.

On the subject of early recognition, she adds; "Any delays in the diagnostic process and subsequent provision will magnify the already existing problems…" There are many other examples available. Parents need to know as quickly as possible to research then choose the most appropriate school or program for their child. That may entail a house move and/or a career or role change for someone in the family. Schools need to know in plenty of time so they can plan for the child's admission and education schedule. The ideal education platform for any student of whatever age, ability or gender, whether they are autistic or NT is low-ratio, student-centered learning. That is, a pupil-teacher ratio of no more than six to one and emphasis should not be to pigeon- hole pupils into subjects or grades, but to expose them to the widest possible educational opportunities to discover their strengths and then build on those. Everyone has a thing or things they do best, this should be nurtured and time not wasted on pushing students to achieve minimum grades in things they hate. The only results of this pernicious, State-imposed philosophy is a leveling Down of education, creating bored, angry, frustrated students whose talents are ignored and who will react negatively to the experience, increased truancy rates will be just one manifestation of that.

    The result for society as a whole of such a policy will be that education will be disdained, good teachers will leave and mediocrity, de-skilling, "dumbing down" and social failure will accelerate. Michelangelo always said of his sculptures that his secret was to "see" the already perfect, realized work within the raw block of marble and to then, with his chisel, reveal that perfection to the world. That is how education should work, to reveal the inner talents and why my argument for Individual Learning/Employment plans is so important for both the individual and society as a whole. The idea that one curriculum or style fits all pupils is nonsense; we are all individuals and should be treated as such. If online or home learning works best for a pupil-great, the tradition of the sardine-school environment should not be considered in any way sacrosanct.

    That strange, eccentric child/employee, usually sitting alone in a corner, perhaps trying to attract attention might just be another Leonardo or Bill Gates and until governments, psychologists and teachers take that on board, education and social systems will fail to maximize their potential-don't blame it on the child. It is probably why many talented students drop out of school at various ages and why a lot of HFAs become self-taught (Autodidacts). To return to Special Education Needs which tends to focus all its resources on people with learning difficulties, let us not forget, as is frequently the case, those at the other end of the spectrum, the highly gifted or genius children. They are as much Special Needs as their less gifted peers. In mainstream education they are often bored, can be disruptive, bullied and their talents stifled by the imposed rigid "curriculum" system, for Aspies this exaggerates their natural tendency to leave tasks/projects uncompleted-they got bored or distracted by something else- gentle guidance can overcome this Aspie trait and foster good habits. A question worth asking of any school is "Have the teachers achieved certified skill levels in "active listening"? It is an important guide to school quality.

If the answer is "yes" it's indicative of a good school, if not, avoid it. "Active listening" is a skill every teacher should have and is especially important in SEN staff. "Active listening" is the ability to understand what is being communicated, not only by mouth but by NVC to the extent of being able to give questioning feedback, explanation and reassurance, demonstrating that the teacher really has grasped the full input and meaning from the pupil and not just nodded through the motions of pretending to be on board-it's about the hallmark of a really good teacher, that desire to go the extra mile for his/her pupils. Gifted is, by definition not "normal". I urge parents to have their child's IQ assessed as early as possible at ages 2, 5, 7, 12 and 15, as some develop their gifts earlier or later than others. The same necessary pre-planning applies equally to these children, their carers and in later life as adults, for self and group advocacy it is an absolute imperative. The alternative for the majority is to be ignored or marginalized

These same criteria apply to all branches of any social or community services available. The earlier they know the better prepared they can be. This must include the local Doctor, the police- who through lack of training and experience can sometimes be grossly abusive or oblivious towards Autists whose unresponsiveness they misinterpret as guilt or defiance, when they simply do not understand the situation. Autistic people are therefore more likely than average to be involved in truancy, petty crime, parking offenses, graffiting and the general thing of not understanding the accepted "Social boundaries" of behavior. Their trusting natures make them the perfect patsies and victims if they get into the wrong circle of people, a fact which a number of law enforcement, social and judicial systems either don't appreciate or simply don't consider.

      The huge number of autistic people who have been fooled or bullied into confessing crimes they did not commit is shocking. To use just two cases from England to illustrate the situation: Firstly that of Barry George, freed after eight years in prison -for the murder of a TV presenter, Jill Dando, a crime he did not commit- having been falsely convicted because he was an easy target for a police force under media pressure to get someone quickly, the victim being a high-profile and popular figure. Regrettably he is not the only one Another is Gary McKinnon, the Scotsman who is both profoundly Asperger's and a computer wizard, who accidentally accessed the wrong US government computer files while searching for information on free energy, flying saucers and "little green men". For this-and it must be stressed he did no harm-he was arrested by the UK police in 2002 and then indicted by a Grand Jury in America and spent years under arrest trying to avoid that government's attempts to extradite him to America where he faced 70 years in jail.

In October 2012 a new British Home Secretary, Theresa May bravely blocked the extradition after advice from top Psychologists revealed that as an Aspie, McKinnon was highly likely to commit suicide if sent to America. He was not malicious, but simply a man unable to grasp the political and judicial implications of his admittedly illegal actions. Would someone with a physical disability, such as failing vision who continued to drive after being advised by a doctor not to do so, have been treated so harshly? McKinnon has now had all charges against him dropped.

Autist and Aspie fact: Dr Venkatesan (of whom much more later) has understood and campaigned about something which few others have either considered or understood; that children and adults with Autism, unlike those with, for example Cerebral Palsy are not necessarily any less disabled, it's only that the disability is not immediately obvious on the outside and people either ignore or fail to see it and feel free to mock, discriminate or bully at will. It is as noxious a behavior to disrespect a person with a learning disability or Autism as it would be to treat a polio victim or amputee like that. Social services need to know about autistic children and adults as soon as possible be able to maximize the help available, as does the NAS in England or the ASA in America along with similar organizations elsewhere in the world, like ASPECT- Autism Spectrum Australia. Families and friends likewise need to know as early as possible, so that they too can plan and learn well in advance, as with any child. Even with genetic testing, which can only, so far provide a statistical likelihood, formal diagnosis is very difficult before the age of two. Now that those genetic tests, those on Chromosome 6 being an example have become available due to an improvement in both scientific equipment and techniques combined with an increased understanding of the cause and effect relationship between certain sequences and Autistic conditions; they are getting closer to the point of being available as part of regular pre-natal screening in the same way as Down's syndrome or Cerebral Palsy screens are routinely conducted today in many countries. Of course pre-natal screening raises many moral, religious and ethical matters which are fully acknowledged, but outside the scope of this book.

Dyslexia Fact: Dyslexia affects males and females in exactly the same ratio as autism does, yet again adding more evidence towards Dyslexia being, at least in many instances part of the Autism Family, rather than the NLD one. However I reserve some considerable doubt about that Dyslexia figure in isolation. Although Chromosome 6 has been positively identified as the carrier of a specific Dyslexic gene, experience suggests that is an incomplete picture for, as Professor Robert Plomin of King's College, London has proved- it is and probably not by coincidence- also a high "intelligence gene". There can, however be no doubt that Chromosome 6 pre-disposes the male to Dyslexia should any of the "triggers" express it. Dyslexia Tip: There are now available a great many electronic aids to help dyslexics from voice controlled typing, to auto-text reader Apps and others, all of which are available on mobile devices as well as desk and laptop computers, they are being improved all the time. Another aid which about a third of dyslexics found helpful (including the author) is Irlen Sheets. They are usually A4 size colored plastic sheets which you place over the text, letter, newspaper etc. and they really can clarify it, although why is not entirely clear. They are cheap and come in a huge range of colors; you pick out the color which best suits your dyslexia and…magic☺.

    The conclusion to this chapter has to be to again restate the importance of early diagnosis to afford the time to prepare the correct type and amount of any interventions required to give the child or adult involved the best chance of maximizing both their lifetime potential and personal happiness. There may indeed not always be a need for intervention in every case, but what every case does, without exception is implore and demand is both acceptance and understanding from friends, family, authorities and society at large. Early diagnosis gives the time to ensure that the conditions for the autistic person are optimized for all those involved at all stages of their lives. In the next chapter we'll examine the two very different psychological interpretations of the mindset of an Autist, following that, the final section of the book will look at a number of practical and sometimes very simple methods, both mainstream and from personal experience to both further explain and enrich the world of autism. To be frank, that world is seldom easy, but with some patience, knowledge, practice, imagination and determination, it can be made a lot easier to navigate than it was only a very few years ago. That section will take a look at the future and the almost miraculous nature of the prospects which are beginning to bloom for autistics and their carers from the fields of science, psychology and education.

Tip:

Adult Employment: Statistically no doubt because of their weak interpersonal skills and spirit of independence-of wanting to do things "their way"- Autists often become successful by being either completely self-employed or freelance contractors who pick and choose their assignments, in the main they are not team players. Another Autistic trait, odd sleeping patterns, preferring or naturally having to sleep during the day has been turned successfully to advantage by some Autists. Many now choose night work, it is easier to find as fewer people want to do night shifts, it pays far better, there is a wider choice of work, commuting is quicker with less traffic and the night is quieter. Autistic night workers can be a valuable asset for employers as they will be sharp and alert at times when NT employees will be flagging or dozing off. A friend who is an ambulance driver is one Autist, and another who is in security chose his work very carefully with his strengths and moral commitment in the forefront of his mind.

Chapter 12

Two views on Asperger's:

Professor Baron-Cohen and his colleagues at the Autism Research Centre at Cambridge University conduct a number of online and face-to-face tests, interviews and surveys from a broad range of volunteers, Aspie or not and regardless of age, education, employment and gender to increase their knowledge and understanding of the Aspie consciousness and mind in comparison with the population at large. One such test consists of around 30 pictures of people's faces, some are full neck-up images, others just brow to nose, emphasizing the expression of the eyes. The volunteers have to select from a list which emotion they think each face is expressing. The greater the number the volunteer gets correct, the higher is rated their emotional "empathy quotient". A second test is written; the volunteer is presented with around 60 statements and asked to express his or her agreement or disagreement with each with the same empathy objective as the picture test. I score below average on facial recognition and above average with textual empathy, illustrating the complexity and multi-facetness of Autism/AS, because images and text are processed by different areas of the brain.

Author's Note: In short; Aspies can't "read" people's faces or voices, and vice versa, that is what the author terms "The NT communication Void" (Hale) and what leads to social mis or non-communication.

From the results of such tests and years of other extraordinarily detailed and deep scientific research, Prof Baron-Cohen has arrived at his startling twin theories, The Empathy Systematizing Theory (EST) and The Extreme Male Brain Theory (EMBT) which are connected closely with his Fetal Testosterone (FT) Theory to form an organic window into the world of an Aspie, whether male or female. Firstly it has long been established by a number of scientists, Baron-Cohen among them, that the "Extreme Female Brain Theory (EFBT) also exists, (Baron-Cohen, S. (2003). The essential difference: male and female brains and the truth about autism. Such a person will be very empathic and caring towards the emotions, feelings and needs of others and will react to those exceptionally well, a care or aid worker perhaps, or kindergarten teacher, all of which statistically trend toward being female-dominated characteristics and spheres. A possible reason for EFBT could be fetal exposure to excess Estrogen-the female hormone- in the womb (Hale).

    During his and others' tests Baron-Cohen found that on average, males-regardless of Asperger's, age or culture -score lower on empathy tests than their female counterparts. He also found that Aspie males score lowest of all within their non-Aspie peer group and that Aspie females also display notably less empathy than their non- Aspie female counterparts, in fact their scores closely resemble those of males, which is part of the reason that Professor Baron-Cohen has cited Asperger's Syndrome as producing the extreme male brain-in either gender. Aspies are not considered to be empaths, and as we have discussed earlier Prof Baron-Cohen ascribes that Aspie brain development, again in either gender to excess embryonic exposure to Testosterone all of which forms his strong, well-evidenced and logical conclusion.

On the other side of the Empathizing-Systematizing Theory, Baron Cohen and his team found that lack of empathy was counter-balanced to a greater or lesser degree by an above average ability to systematize and that Aspies are the most systematic of all, again regardless of gender. "Systematic" in this context refers to the aptitude with which an individual analyzes, organizes, interprets and understands the operation of how systems, logic and processes work; car mechanics, science, program writing, surgery and film-making are good examples of systematics, in which traditionally at least, men do better than women.

To take programming, the process of creating algorithms is extremely detailed and systematic- Aspies excel in both those disciplines. Examples include, Alfred Hitchcock, chemist Henry Cavendish, Sir Isaac Newton, Charles Darwin, Jane Austen, Thomas Edison, Apple founder Steve Jobs, Face book founder, Mark Zuckerberg is rumored to be an Aspie, Henry Ford was, the chess-master Bobby Fischer, Abraham Lincoln, English writer Virginia Woolf, Vernon Smith and the genius physicist and creator of the "Many Worlds Theory" of cosmology, Professor Hugh Everett 111, who was also the father of the famous musician, Mark Everett, founder of the band, The Eels. Some of these Aspie HFAs we have already met, some are new friends, all of whom add ever more credibility to the theory.

All Aspie geniuses have one thing in common, it's as if they have multiple programs going on in their heads and they are brilliant at more than one thing and are able to focus, often to the point of obsession on each one in turns. Those things may seem contradictory; Newton was a genius physicist, mathematician, Theologian and Alchemist, Leonardo, a painter, architect, military engineer, pioneer map-maker and more. To all HFA Aspies, thought is a continual desire to "connect the dots", to seek patterns and produce a greater revelation of what makes up the world, finding the order in its apparent chaos. Einstein's lifelong and unfinished struggle to find the Grand Unified Theory (GUT) of physics- the formula which would balance the four Fundamental forces of The Universe- is one example and a primary Aspie diagnostic criterion as well as being another constituent of why, like Leonardo, Aspies find completing projects so difficult. They get diverted easily, the "Minds like a butterfly" trap. It is something Aspies need to both recognize within themselves and address, as it's primarily their responsibility and problem and they first need to face up to it. Without guidance it is next to impossible and all Autists can be extremely stubborn, infuriatingly so-Autists aren't saints by any stretch of the imagination and being angry or despairing at them from time to time is natural, understandable and Autists get angry with each other too, it's all part of being human. No one is perfect and there is no shame in that.

Another Perspective:

There are naturally several theories about Autism/AS, to list them all would be a very lengthy and frequently repetitive task, as many are variations of each other to a greater or lesser degree. That is not so with the second major "stand alone" theory; The Neanderthal Theory of Autism. Neanderthals were so named after their first remains were uncovered in the Neander valley near Düsseldorf, Germany. Over the last century, thanks to hard, dedicated efforts by both individuals and groups in the fields of practical Archaeology in retrieving physical evidence of Mankind's past and forensic archaeologists for the scientific analysis of those finds, including the usage of DNA sequencing and profiling techniques, we now have a finely detailed, if still incomplete picture of humanity and its history.

These individuals include Sir Arthur Evans who found the great palace of Knossos on the Greek isle of Crete, Gertrude Bell who uncovered much of our history and knowledge of ancient Jerusalem, Professor Heinrich Schliemann, discoverer of the legendary city of Troy in modern Turkey and the Spanish engineer Rocque Joaquin de Alcibierre who excavated the buried Roman town of Pompeii. By combining their results and anecdotal evidence with that obtained by physicists, bio-physicists, historians and biochemists, science has achieved a very new and clearer picture of the development and origins of us, modern humans (homo sapiens), it is somewhat different from what was thought until very recently. Modern Man is currently considered to be only about 160,000-300,000 years old (New Scientist, June 11th, 2003) Whichever end of that timeline is correct the fact is that at one point we and our genetically close cousins, Neanderthal man co-existed across substantial regions of our planet for many tens of millennia. Their origin goes back at least 600,000 years.

It was long thought that we caused the extinction of Neanderthals within a short while of meeting them, now though the latest archeological and genetic information shows that not only did the two Man-types share land, but also sporadically interbred for tens of thousands of years, until only some 30,000 years ago, when Neanderthal suddenly and mysteriously disappeared (National Geographic, May 6th, 2010). This idea of inter-breeding was dismissed by the majority of scientists as lacking sufficient evidence. Then in March 2013 the skeleton of a child, a proven hybrid of human and Neanderthal was discovered in Northern Italy dating back about 40, 000BP (Before Present), the Theory now looks much stronger.

This study was conducted by Prof Ed Green and his team at the University of Santa Cruz in California and backed up a long-held opinion by Anthropologists. This combination has given rise to the Neanderthal Theory of Autism. Some (but not all) of us to this day share somewhere between 1 and 4 percent of our DNA with Neanderthal, and as we have seen with genetics, a little bit of cause may result in very big effects, as we will examine in the following chapter. Parts of that DNA, both regular and mitochondrial contain many of the combinations which we now believe to be associated with Autism and especially Asperger's in ourselves. It is found most commonly in specific ethnic groups, the most prominent being the Basques from an area straddling France and Spain and one of my paternal germ-lines. To understand the potential of the theory it is necessary in the light of recent discoveries in archeology to radically re-evaluate what Neanderthal man was really like, as compared with his previously "brutish" media-established public image and how that may tie-in with Baron-Cohen's theory. Firstly, they had bigger brains and bodies than modern Man, (as did Cro-Magnons-size isn't everything☺, they were pale-skinned and often had reddish hair, their extraordinary cave art pre-dates ours by at least 4,000 years as discovered by Dr Alistair Pike of Bristol University in the UK, who found the oldest known cave art in El Castillo, Spain, dating back more than forty thousand years which is described in a Bristol University press release, June 14th, 2012.

They invented games, played carved-bone musical instruments, held elaborate burial ceremonies for their dead, complete with flowers, food, clothes, jewelry and tools, which strongly suggests that they believed in an existence beyond physical death as much as the ancient Egyptians did, millennia later. They built permanent homes from the bones of giant mammoths, after previously being cave-dwellers (The Daily Telegraph December 18th, 2011). Skeletal remains indicate they suffered from modern types of cancer and also that they could speak and would have done so with a high, slightly warbling voice-far removed from their media depiction as grunting savages.

    Neanderthals were wide-ranging hunters, using caves mainly as hunting lodges, but only rarely nomadic in lifestyle, unless external conditions forced it upon them, which would have made them very in-tune with nature, both animals, plants and the seasons compared with the more gathering and then farming-based societies of Homo sapiens. They lived in small, family/kin-based groups, as opposed to the more cosmopolitan and social Human, who quickly learned to live in larger, settled communities, villages, towns and then cities. This would mean, in terms of evolution and the survival imperative that Neanderthal did not need the same degree of social and interpersonal skills which we take for granted today, but did need to be more aware of and "at one" with nature, both of which are strongly Autistic and particularly Aspie traits, which may be significant clues in the makeup of the autism picture.

      Like almost all non-human species of animal of whatever type, it is proposed that like Aspies, Neanderthals did not make frequent eye-contact with others, again unlike modern Man. Like their other contemporaries, us and Cro-Magnon-Man they used flint tools to cut wood, carve and prepare meat and pelts for food and clothing. This also suggests they knew how to cook and shave and were therefore at least as intelligent and dexterous as ourselves at that time (EarthSci). Until 2010 it was assumed that they inhabited only the cold, northerly regions of Europe but now that their remains have been found in Spain, France and modern Italy by an archeological team from the University of Denver in Colorado, we see that they, like us were an adaptable people. Beyond that we know very little of them. However, from their cave art and carving an intriguing observation has been made: its technique, application and composition were found to resemble very closely those of the modern Autistic/AS Savant artists, adding further value to the Neanderthal-Autism theory.

**Neanderthal Man
ca. 600,000 bp**

My own DNA analysis has revealed a very high above 3% of Neanderthal DNA. As an experiment I have re-sat Simon's empathy-photograph test, yet with various animal faces and voices chosen by random people from their own varied sources, books, magazines and photographs of animals in different situations, happy, in pain, aggressive, bored and so on-which were revealed to the person taking the test only after they had completed it. They found pictures of dogs, horses, cats, elephants, rabbits, cows and many more; I then invited Aspie friends, volunteers and colleagues to do the same test.

For me and the majority of the other Aspies who score below average with human empathy, we scored well above average using Simon's criteria when the faces were those of animals. Of course this only suggests an idea, because the sample size of people was too small to be scientifically valid. Still, it is nonetheless interesting, as more than seventy Aspies have done it to date, with nearly 66% reflecting a higher score with animal than with human images-very Neanderthal, perhaps? In over twenty-five years of professional experience I have unquestionably seen that Auties/Aspies do display an unusual empathy, gentleness and affection for the natural world as a whole and animals in particular compared with many of their NT contemporaries, this embracement of nature is an important and much under-valued quality in this industrialized and polluted day and age. Empathy in Professor Baron's Cohen's work refers principally to the ability to interpret and relate to another person's feelings and situation; these are usually expressed by voice tonality, facial expression and body language, Aspies are not good at any of these which may explain their trend towards being socially isolated. Aspies are frequently described as "loners", at least by the media. That though is an over-simplification; the reality is that although they do like their privacy and a low-stimulation environment more than most, few are as such by choice, but are neglected or "left alone" by mainstream society; people seldom choose to be lonely.

  Furthermore it must be made clear that the words "empathy", "sensitivity", "sympathy" and compassion" are not synonyms and that Aspies are strongly capable of those emotions-the great foundation set up by Bill and Melinda Gates is a case in point. Newton's famous love of animals and nature-he was the inventor of the cat-flap- and Van Gogh's compassion for the human condition are leading excellent examples. My feeling is that Aspies have as much depth of emotion as anyone, but for different things, that is to say a different and narrower but not shallower emotional bandwidth. Author's conjecture: On the face of things this fact alone would seem, along with the artistic and religious depth of Neanderthals to put our two theories almost in complete opposition with each other but perhaps that may not be the case at all. I believe they are both valuable pieces in an as yet incomplete picture of Asperger's.

Neanderthals being bigger and stronger than us must have possessed a more powerful endocrine system than our own, one able to produce at the very least the potency and volume of the growth hormones needed to achieve their size. It follows that it must be considered that they did the same for other hormones, including Testosterone in both genders. Parts of the differences in their and our DNA would account for that, maybe they had a sequence instruction or specific genes to "make lots of hormones". If and it would be in very rare instances, the testosterone code of that mechanism is inherited by a modern Homo Sapien, that could explain the FT theory in practicevNormally in order for an inherited genetic condition to express in a child it needs a copy of that gene from both parents-hemophilia is an exception, Wilson's disease and Tay-Sachs are just two of the more typical Autosomal recessive category.

Suppose that Asperger's is in that category and that both parents would need the right Neanderthal copies to produce the unusually high FT levels pivotal to Prof Baron-Cohen's theory? Such a situation would confirm his theory and explain why Asperger's is so uncommon. Even if it took only one parent with the right

Neanderthal DNA to produce high FT levels, that would still be a very unlikely circumstance and the theory would remain fully intact.

"As we already know, just the presences of any particular genes do not guarantee their expression. Perhaps for even the minority with Neanderthal DNA it normally remains dormant.....for whatever reasons, unless, it is "triggered" by some as yet unknown factor(s)-perhaps even by the partner also having Neanderthal DNA or some environmental fluctuation. It seems to me that there are quite a few combinations which would synergize both theories and in so doing greatly expand both our knowledge and assumptions to date. It is research which needs to be done, not only for AS, but to increase our understanding of our past and the workings of our human Genome in general" (Hale, 2013).

Psychological Fact: All people dream during sleep whether they remember the dreams or not and that includes blind people. These fall into two categories broadly: those who were born blind (congenital blindness) or became blind very young and those who lose their sight at a later stage, typically after the age of 5. The dreams of the young-blind contain only a very few and indistinct images, but a magical, subtle rainbow of sounds. The later-blind dream with much the same image intensity as the normally-sighted and with little aural enhancement. This relates to autism as a "whole body condition" by again showing us the overlap between the physical and the mental and asks us searching questions about how we define, perceive and interpret that relationship in modern psychiatric practice.

Chapter 13

The "Whole Body Condition":

This penultimate chapter is about the nature of Autism/AS and how it can be interpreted to everyone's increased advantage and comfort. We know that its principle visible effects are in the socio-cognitive area and beyond that from the Autism Family that its less obvious results extend far further to affect the whole body and mind in a myriad of different ways, subtle and otherwise. The absolute cornerstone in the true understanding of Autism/AS is to realize that it is primarily a physical condition, not a mental one. The observed psychological presentations are caused by structural variances within the brain, which in turn affect the whole body, that is why there are the distinct physical conditions associated with it, such as gut and stomach problems, Tuberous Sclerosis and Fragile X Syndrome-some of the Co-morbid conditions on our Tree. These apply whether the autism is inherited or induced at a later stage of life, as determined previously.

This is perhaps the most important point the book seeks to make: that those with ASDs experience life completely differently from the NT community and that society's approach and attitude to Autism in all its forms needs to both change and expand in order to take full account of that truth. Many Autists see life as a series of individual tableaux, rather than a continuous "work in progress"; building up a library of experience to be applied or called upon as required. This is why Aspies tend to be naive and easily exploited as we have seen. Some have phenomenal memories, leading others to believe that Autists frequently make things up.

Many are very imaginative and creative, again leading to them being disbelieved and their input under-appreciated or not understood at all. This type of rejection dogged Prof Everett for much of his career-he was simply "too far ahead of his time" and a whole generation had to pass before his theorems were taken seriously, a situation which naturally made him depressed and led to him to bouts of alcoholism and an early death at the age of 51. It not too strong to say that society's ignorance and attitudes was directly responsible for Everett's death and furthermore illustrates the fine line between the physical and the emotional.

The touchstone proof of the nature of a "whole body condition" lies in the basic philosophy of modern clinical practice, namely Evidence Based Medicine (EBM), which dates back about 150 years. The idea is that clinical and psychological "Best Practice" is evolved by taking as much evidence from statistics, respectable publications and studies from around the world as possible to make a sort of semi- ad hoc manual of the best and most successful approaches and treatment for each patient with any specific condition or conditions.

The WHO provide us with an extensive guide, "World Best Practice", (WBP) based on their findings and the EBM philosophy.

There are, unfortunately a number of conflicts inherent in this system of which we need to be aware; one of which is in the selection of the "evidence" itself, some which may be falsified, as in the Wakefield case or in conflict with current establishment positions in any country and so get ignored, some may be overlooked or misunderstood due to ignorance, some may simply be wrong and some omitted because the financial implications of carrying out WBP are politically unacceptable due to cost-the reality of the infamous "profit before people" culture-whether in private or State health provision. The best advice to all patients and carers is to research your regional policies and record them thoroughly and then ask doctors lots of questions. Good doctors will be happy to answer; bad ones will refuse or be evasive.

One example of a failing in EBM practice stems from the differences of opinion on which evidence is used and from when and where. The WHO sets the correct precedents by continually updating its advice as the latest findings emerge once they are verified. The same applies to the Life Extension Foundation of Fort Lauderdale, Florida, a non-profit organization, whose research; practice and positive contribution to good health worldwide cannot be praised too highly. It was started by Saul Kent and William Falcon in 1980 and now ranks as one of the finest and most accessible medical institutes in the world with a virtual "Who's Who" of top clinicians being actively involved. I recommend all their publications to anyone with an interest in personal or public health. To give an illustration of this potential divergence of WBP from EBM we need only look at the question of how Blood test ranges differ from country to country, even some of those with clinically advanced facilities. This is because there is no one enforceable standard which the evidence in EBM has to meet. If the evidence upon which any particular region or country is basing their practice is wrong or outdated then the whole process of EBM theory works against and not for the patient and that happens in today's world. There are still systems which use ranges outdated by more than 60 years when assessing blood, hormone, allergy/food intolerance patterns and pathogen (germ) panels, the UK being an example.

These old ranges were designed as "a healthy minimum" meaning in cold cynical terms that the patient was just functional enough to work, not that he/she was in good health. The same is true of other diagnostic shortcuts, X-rays for example are used for cheapness where MRI scanning would provide better, more detailed information and as a result a better outcome for the patient. The spurious justification is, "we've been using X-rays for over a hundred years", on that argument practitioners should (and actually do in some Practices) withhold certain life-saving medicines because they are deemed "too new", crazy thinking-that would include antibiotics. "Correct practice would be to base all test ranges for any population on the readings from elite athletes, doing this would force the medical sector to improve overall health by spurring them to treat ambitiously up towards a target, not down conveniently, to a price" (Hale 2012). It is a continuing scandal that in certain wealthy countries ordinary people are still denied both life-saving and life-enhancing care on grounds of cost and any doctor who accedes to such a situation is by definition "unfit to practice" and should be criminally liable. Another type of doctor to avoid-and there are a few, too many to list fully here- is "Dr backhander" he/she is delighted to accept cash, holiday vouchers, goods and other "services" from certain disreputable drug companies in return for prescribing their products, irrespective of patient need or safety.

Then there is perhaps the worst type of all health service practitioners; namely those with the attitude, consciously or subconsciously that "medical technology and progress reached its peak the day I got my diploma" and have never bothered to keep upgrading their skills since, you find these fossils of various ages, dotted right across the medical spectrum, killing or otherwise failing as many patients today through arrogance and laziness as they did thirty years ago through ignorance. The best advices are to "look, listen and learn" and always seek a second opinion if possible. Look at the practice or hospital- does it seem clean, modern and motivated? Listen to other patients and carers' experiences. Research and learn both about the doctor and the medical issues with which you're concerned, again from text books, journals or high quality internet sites, with PubMed, the LEF and WebMD being among the best. The majority of doctors are of course very good so it is worth taking the time to spot the few bad ones, the same point applies to clinics, hospitals and the psychiatric sector

Important Autistic/Aspie Fact: Auties and Aspies do not return "normal" clinical test-range results, our bodies are different, especially in the areas of yeast infection (Candida) allergies and food intolerance response, all of which trend towards underlying autoimmune conditions-those conditions where the immune system attacks its own healthy cells instead of external pathogens- (germs) Rheumatoid Arthritis being one such condition, as well as the more

Autism-specific ones we shall look at in Chapter 14. Allergies and Autism are both cross-linked to an increased risk of migraine headaches (Mayo Clinic). It is vital to find a specialist who understands that and can therefore interpret any results correctly (Autismtoday.com, July-August 2004-Shaw, W). The same principle applies to other areas; "normal" body temperature being one, it differs between some Auties/AS and NTs and your physician should be made aware of this. It is this type of newly emerging evidence which again highlights Autism as a "whole body condition".

Another Savant artist: Born severely autistic, Stephen Wilshire from London, England was sent to a Special Needs School, where having previously been unable to speak (a "mute") he uttered his first word at the age of nine. He is now one of the world's greatest line draughtsmen. He can look at any object, person, land or cityscape once and reproduce it on paper exactly, which has given rise to his nickname, "The human camera". It is vital to be "drug and substance-aware" for Autists and Aspies as well as food aware, as they react atypically from the average person. Some Aspies can't tolerate common prescription (and non-prescription) meds, some need higher or lower dosages of what they can tolerate, making it yet more important to have an informed practitioner because Aspies frequently "self-medicate" with a variety of things, looking for "the normal" or at least some peace of mind somehow. For this reason the author suggests strongly that Autistics wear a "Medic Alert" identification tag at all times. On the subject of drugs and the general population it is poor practice that some doctors give out "one size fits all" dosages. 1000mg a day of Y may be fine for a 200 Lb. 40 year old male but is likely to prove an overdose for a 110 Lb., 18 year old female. Often adverse reactions, failures and side effects stem from thoughtless mis-dosing, despite the drug company's very specific and detailed guidelines to doctors. The hospital practice of prescribing by age, gender and gm. /mg per kilo, per patient is the proper, safer practice.

Returning to one of this book's early points, autistic people process their inner as well as the outer world very differently from the NT majority as Einstein among others explain. Auties/AS do not see color, taste food, hear, feel emotion, sense, speak or touch as do others, some of these things they may do better or worse or just differently from the normal. Take Einstein's brain, which he donated to medical research in his Will.bWithin a few hours of his death in

April 1955 a pathologist had removed and dissected it into 240 cubes, taking many hundreds of photographs while he worked, many unpublished until recently and now partially digitally reconstructed.

These images have now been made available and provide compelling evidence about the nature of both autism and genius. Firstly size is not important, Einstein's brain was a little smaller than average, however its physical structure, even what we have seen so far was very different from "normal", exhibiting as we would expect, marked differences and more complex connections especially in the prefrontal area which is crucial for thinking and spatial perception. He could construct concepts and pictures in his mind which others could not. The same can be said of autistic Savant, Temple Grandin, whose brain, it has been revealed by tests and scans published in 2012, is both larger, especially the left lobe (which ties in neatly with Dr Cahill's findings at Irvine) than average and quite structurally different in many ways. Furthermore her actual electro-chemical connections, "the wiring" of her brain is as unusual as are her extraordinary abilities in the fields of reading, memory, spelling, pure thinking, sense of space and logical reasoning.

She is a professor at Colorado University; a doctor of animal sciences and behavior, a famous inventor, author of The Learning style for people with autism, 1995 among many publications, a left-hander and a standard-bearer for the early diagnosis and interventional approaches to maximize the life potential of Autists and Aspies everywhere as well as a strong autism rights advocate. She also has weaknesses; predictably in the emotional sides of life, which are again explained by her unusual brain, where areas and connections associated with emotion and the ability to identify faces and facial expressions are weak by comparison with the average.

For further hard scientific evidence towards understanding the nature of the Whole Body Condition we need to take a closer look at the various types of imaging and brain function monitoring techniques now available, some of which were used in Prof Grandin's case because they reveal the intricacies and workings of the human mind both in its NT and non-NT manifestations. The most common form of imaging is the old X-ray method; the earliest form of so-called "nuclear medicine" as it relies entirely on radioactive waves penetrating the body to form the plate. However it produces only two dimensional results, which although fine for detecting broken bones and foreign objects, lacks both the detail and resolution necessary for accurate situational analysis.

It's more complex successor is the CT (Computerized Tomography), machine which fires multi-directional X-rays from all round the patient simultaneously in "slices, which can vary in thickness down to 1mm for fine detail. These slices are then reassembled by computer CAT-Computer Axial Tomography - to produce detailed 3 dimensional views which are a huge aid in all branches of medicine. For scanning complex organs like the liver, stomach or brain "contrast CTs" may be ordered. In this procedure a type of dye is injected into the patient before the scan to "highlight" the area(s) under investigation for even higher accuracy and resolution.

CT scanning is the most popular form of advanced non-invasive investigation because; despite its disadvantages it is highly effective and a lot cheaper than the alternative not just in operation but in terms of the initial cost of the equipment. That said, with those inherent dangers I cannot fully endorse their use where a better option is available. The principle concern is that people tend to need a number of scans-regardless of the type used- and each CT scan contains approximately the same level of radiation as 500 or more conventional X-rays leading to an increased risk of cancers developing in patients who need frequent scans. The second potential hazard is that some patients may develop anaphylactic shock as a reaction to the contrast material, although this is rare because good hospitals carry out thorough pre-scan tests.

A better and inevitably more expensive method is the MRI scan, using similar computer tomography but with magnetic waves instead of X-rays, they are not cancer-causers (Carcinogens) and because they differentiate better between hard and soft tissue like bone or muscle-again building a 3D picture in slices (something akin to the way the seabed is mapped by SONAR) - they provide a sharper higher quality picture of the area being scanned, making them particularly useful for brain imaging.

In both types of scan the person lies very still in a kind of large very noisy plastimetal cigar tube, which can be very claustrophobic. Some people find it easier to have a small dose of a tranquillizer, usually Diazepam before a scan, which also helps them remain motionless throughout the process which is hard to do, but necessary for the best results. Scans can seem frightening, especially for young children, but there really is nothing to fear when they are done properly by a good hospital or clinic. As with CTs a contrast material can be used for even greater resolution (with the same risk) but is needed less often, safeguarding more patients.

These scanning techniques have revolutionized our understanding of the human brain and have given us unimpeachable evidence that the structure and operational method of the autistic/AS brain is quantifiably different from non-autistic ones. This has been re-confirmed using an even more modern technique, the functional MRI (f MRI). This allows the actual flow of blood to the brain to be watched in real-time and in color, the procedure itself is the same as the standard MRI, except that a unique contrast material is used. By observing blood flow, it shows which areas of the brain are most activated by what kind of stimulus. Combined with EEG monitoring they give us a very clear working map of where everything is and what it does, for instance the center which processes sight; enabling us to see.

An EEG is an Electroencephalograph. It monitors the electrical activity in the brain-the brain receives information, processes it and gives the appropriate responses by means of biochemically generated electrical signals-we are electric beings. To understand the idea it is worth thinking of the brain, human or animal as a kind of electro-chemically etched-(imprinted) 4D multi-layer, squidgy (im) printed-circuit board. By following the electric current pathways, we can see which stimuli produce which result in any part of the brain, images, music, smells and so on. Autistic brains display different electrical "maps" from those of NTs. Alternatively we can compare the brain with an old-fashioned telephone exchange, where Autistic brains connect differently from NT ones.

Each time we experience or learn something it forms a new etched pathway on the brain, that is the "soft wiring" of the brain. That applies equally to good and bad experiences, the more intense the experience the quicker and more entrenched the memory will be. These neuron (transmitter electro-chemicals) pathways form easiest while we are young, enabling children to learn many things very fast, multilingualism being one example. On the dark side it is also why childhood traumas can be so life-dominating. By constantly re-enforcing certain behaviors we deepen and sharpen those pathways. That is how learning works, why "practice makes perfect" and why therefore positive learning is so important. It is also explains why people get "stuck in their ways" as they get older, by constant repetition of routine behaviors. To avoid this constantly seek new hobbies and challenges like doing an online course or going to the gym, these help keep the faculties intact and lively, the brain need exercise as well as the body. Those pathways are technically described by Neurologists as "Engrams" and the junctions where they interconnect and relay (Like roundabouts) are Synapses. By knowing this, it is possible by various methods some of which we shall outline in the final chapter to re-program the brain to a more positive operating pattern.

    Brain Fact: Left or right brain dominance: All of us have the two hemispheres (sides) to our brain and one is always dominant. The strengths given by the left brain lie in the areas of logic, math, reasoning, planning, analytic thinking and languages. Those who favor the right brain will be better at recognizing people, have better social and interpersonal skills, a greater appreciation of art, color and music and be more intuitive and creative. The author has been tested and is very left-brain dominant.

To conclude, I strongly believe and assert that Autism is not a pathological state, but an entire "State of being and Consciousness unique of itself".

Chapter 14

Help is at hand:

In addition to the strategies already outlined, fortunately for many but not all Autists, the answer is "quite a lot", far too much to fit into a small guide- but here are a few paths worth exploring; the most important of which are effort, understanding and patience on top of some of the therapies already mentioned like hypnosis, drug treatment, Drama, clinical testing assessment and CBT.

Omega 3 Fish oil is good for everyone, for a fully grown adult the useful amount is approximately 6 mg per Pound of body weight (about 1200mg) for a child under 16, half that. Fish oils act as blood thinners; anyone on prescribed blood thinners should consult their doctor. But the big point is that studies have shown O3 to be a good treatment for some childhood autism and Depression (Biol

Psychiatry. 2007 Feb 15; 61(4):551-3), as well as helping to keep arteries clearer of plaques, lessening the risk of some cancers, heart disease and Dementia, reducing acne, inflammation in general (including in the gut) and arthritis in particular among many other benefits. It is a supplement I use daily along with Vitamin E and Chamomile or Green tea.

    Nootropics: a.k.a. "Smart drugs" and supplements. A whole new generation of drugs and supplements, some derived from natural elements, others laboratory synthesized, which nourish the natural chemicals of the brain, improving memory, speed of thought and intelligence. These are applicable to everyone. They are still mostly first generation preparations and their long-term benefits/hazards are as yet not known. Current popular ones are L-Carnatine, O3, Vitamin B groups, Vitamin D, 5-HTP, SAM-e, DHEA, Piracetum, Modafinil, CDP-Choline, CO Q10 and Folic Acid to name but a few. Separately, there are being developed electronic devices which can, if they succeed, control brainwave activity to avoid over stimulation and produce the calm waves. They are the Neuro-equivalent of a heart pacemaker. It will be worth checking closely on their progress over the years ahead, through the Transhumanist

Movement's work. The potential is certainly exciting and hopeful. Returning once more to education practice, Ruth Wilson's book Special Educational Needs in the Early Years (Wilson, 2003) is excellent, covering in a comprehensive manner most of the current SEN methods, both for the school and at home. She emphasizes the positive role of learning by play, especially outdoor provision to encourage social skills and interaction with other children. In this structure, the teacher sets up the situation then praises the autistic child at suitable moments when they display positive behavior. By these actions, positive behavior is re-enforced at the earliest stages of development. She points out the need for teachers and social services to encourage parents to continue this method in the home environment. This author has found through his own practice that this method is very effective, with the caveat that it is also very demanding both in terms of teacher concentration and in requiring the very low pupil-teacher ratio already stated in order to be effective.

A second notable point Wilson makes, is how vital it is to provide "Quiet Rooms" or "Time Out Spaces." Autistics are easily upset (among autistics these episodes are known as "melt-downs" and are caused by the brain being overloaded by stimuli-physical or mental and either shutting off, leaving the person frozen or over-reacting by lashing out, usually verbally but sometimes physically as all teachers know. To have a facility to allow them a calm, safe place to recover is very helpful, if the space can provide quiet, soothing music and low light, so much the better. This can take the form of a refuge area away from the demands of the classroom or home and works better than anything else, including drugs in this author's experience of teaching SEN groups in various settings.

      In a similar vein from the University of Mysore in India is Dr S Venkatesan's Children with Developmental Difficulties (Venkatesan, 2004). It is a catalogue of practices, more systematic than Wilson's, but containing less commentary and professional anecdotes. At this point, it is worth noting that not all children with developmental difficulties are Autistic, Downs Syndrome children being one example, but that most SEN methods are equally applicable to most physically able groups. He advocates teaching by small increments of success in a very carefully structured program, a multi-step process towards skill acquisition. He calls the system "Short Term Goal Teaching." The idea is based on the fact that these children have concentration difficulties, so he builds skills, block by block, one small step at a time. He has devised a series of techniques for promoting attention/concentration. He describes one such "For older children, number game activities like forward repetition of digits, presented by the caregiver/teacher at the rate of one number per second, can be carried out to improve concentration." "Another one is the learning of three word sentences by constant repetition both spoken and written". However, like Wilson he too stresses the importance of the family/caregivers in maintaining the system, Dr Venkatesan's reputation for success is renowned.

There are two themes in common with these named authors and others, namely to stress the paramount importance of the role and attitude of the child's/adult's family/caregivers. Perhaps the book which has most influenced this guide in educational terms is Philip Kendall's Childhood Disorders (Psychology Press, 2000). In it he alphabetically and systematically lists each disorder and describes its causes and presentations and the central role in children's lives which parents and other family members involved in the situation or treatment can play. Instead of working one-to-one with child therapists who work with the children, he often chooses to spend at least some time teaching the" parents to work with the child " Not only should we care about the autistic, but also about their supporters. It is they, in combination with teachers who predict the child's future. It must be emphasized on top of this that the first duty of any caregiver in whatever situation is to care for and inform themselves-otherwise they will fail. The second common theme is the agreement in the imperative of early diagnosis to maximize the results.

A teaching method which this author has used for SEN children is Kinesthic teaching, based on Harvard Professor Howard Gardner's ideas on multiple types of intelligence (The Theory of Multiple Intelligences, Gardner, 1983), that were further developed by Dr V Prakash again, at Mysore University. Kinesthetic learning is a teaching and learning style in which learning takes place while the student actually carries out a physical activity, rather than passively sitting, listening to a lecture or watching a demonstration/video. Following on from the "learning through movement" method is the idea of learning through dance, joining a Drama-group or singing Karaoke each is great-for the mind, the body and their ability to build and enhance positive social interactions and patterns. Bodily kinesthetic intelligence is the ability to use the body to express emotion (as in dance and body language), to play games, Autists are naturally-given the chance-playful and keen to create a new product (as in crafts and invention). Through interaction with the spaces around them, students are able to remember and process information more readily. In fact the body instinctively knows and can learn many things which our conscious minds do not and cannot know in any other way, that "muscle memory" is part of every person's array of often untapped talent, whether Autistic or NT. For example, it is how our bodies learn to type, ride a bicycle, stitch a cloth, or skate on rollerblades.

To date my experiences using either Kinesthic or music have both been very successful-and when combined it is the best system there is-not only from an academic perspective-things like learning to count, but for physical health and inner calm. My thing is a combination of Mozart and balloons/beanbags according to the type of group and their age/disability. It is a technique which works great on adults- they have found playing Mozart helps them to conquer exam nerves as well as revise and recall more effectively prior to exams-at every level. I have done the same thing at business seminars-beanbags and Mahler, helps in life/career or goal coaching, is fun and is a great team-building exercise.

Learning with the use of flashcards, shown for one second intervals imparts knowledge virtually unconsciously, this fascinating synergy between the conscious and the unconscious is an area that psychologists and behaviorists have investigated since Freud. The brain alone is not the whole story. Consequently, many students do best while being able to move around and interact with things, boosting their creativity. People tend to lose concentration if there is little or no external stimulus going on. It is useful to employ activities and games which challenge hand-eye co-ordination, some well-supervised indoor sports like table tennis, handball and especially swimming. Swimming is the complete Whole mind and body workout making it perfect for Autists and Aspies alike…and you ☺.

When the brain is challenged it produces increased electro-chemical activity, which in turn aids memory. Incorporating one of the above-mentioned activities into lessons will help pupils take part more completely in the activity and remember the lesson more clearly. For instance, the use of balloons or small, soft beanbags in teaching can present fun challenges. An early exercise would be for two students to face each other and hit the balloon back and forth as quickly as possible with their hands while practicing the alphabet, each student takes a turn saying a letter or word at the instant of hitting the balloon. After practicing that way, the students use their elbow to hit the balloon as they say the letter; then to make it even more challenging the students use their non-dominant elbow, knee or foot to hit the balloon or catch the beanbag, this exercise is an excellent tool. It can be used for learning such things as counting the days of the week, the months, naming fruits, vegetables, flowers, telling the time, learning math tables, phrases, rhymes and sentences, which can be written on a board or projected to augment the "learn-by-eye" response.

Kinesthetic exercises are excellent opportunities to discover, practice, and reinforce learning. They are best when kept simple and purposeful. If an exercise is too complicated students become frustrated and will not learn as much. The exercises should be short, approximately twenty minutes or less for a session and of course, they too, can be done at home.

From experience I will add learning a musical instrument to any level of achievement as one of the best and most enjoyable things anyone can do, even banging two spoons together. Music is a fantastic combination of fun, increasing knowledge, expression and great therapy, perhaps the most famous proponent of which was Albert Einstein with his violin. Learning music is knowledge in itself but it also increases the brain's overall fitness and capacities and as a result it will learn all the other things better as well. Learning to juggle gives a real boost to self-esteem and co-ordination, both of which are traditionally weak areas for Autists. Better still, all these activities tend to be in a group which aids the social and emotional development of the Autist, they are all win-win activities. The secret again is to keep the sessions short enough to remain a joy and not become a chore.

Taking that a stage further brings us to a somewhat controversial topic, "The Mozart Effect" Good music particularly Mozart is cited as the most beneficial. If prospective parents have any autistic genetic history (or even if they don't) ante-natal (before birth) exposure to Mozart, about twenty to thirty minutes twice a day is widely medically recommended – some studies have indicated that it stimulates and activates the vital P (erception) centers in the brain- perhaps increasing innate childhood intelligence by as much as 10% and aiding the ability to both learn and recall in later life. It certainly produces a strong feeling of well-being in mother and child and decreases Depression as well as the marked anxiety so prominent in most forms of Autism.

Pieces by the Austrian composer Gustav Mahler have been shown to act similarly and there may be others as yet un-discovered. The basic fact is that some music can be calming, stimulating and/or healing as sounds (Sonics) have been demonstrated to literally reprogram (by re-etching) the brain pathways in a positive fashion, in the same, but more enjoyable way as Behavioral Therapies, Psycho-active medications and other things do. The secret is to keep trying all the alternatives, initially one at a time and if necessary, in combination until you find the balance which works best for you. It can be a long, hard process and I shall give no false hope or slick, quick, easy promises. All I can say for sure is that Music has at times helped me and others.

Painting, drawing and such activities as clay modeling and knitting are all tools of "Art Therapy" they are well-proven to help some people. The goal of art therapy is not so much to produce great or necessarily even strictly realistic art but internally representative art, although some great artists have been discovered through it. Its real goals are to permit and enable non-verbal communication and emotional expression, to express the inner world to the outer one. This accomplishes both the important tasks, social interaction, trust and the release of, or explanation of distress- the idea that a picture can tell a thousand words- it can explain, not only in action but in technique and choice of colors a great deal about a person's past and present, helping the psychologist to find the best path forward. People and not only Autists and especially the young find it less traumatic to show if they have been bullied or abused in some way, rather than talk about it, even if they were able to do so, remembering that some Autists cannot process words and are unable to talk, making them particularly vulnerable, for them art can be a real lifeline.

The sessions, method and media used can be both flexible and varied, film one day, painting by brush or fingers the next and perhaps a craft approach after that. Some of history's greatest painters like Pablo Picasso and Joseph (WM) Turner frequently painted with their fingers for a more intense and immediate dramatic effect as well as to create different textures on the canvas, true 3D effects. The basic idea is to relieve, reveal and calm the mind. It works.

Other helpful skills are learning Yoga and a Meditation technique-something I have never managed, but a lot of people do and report very positively on the effects for them. Hypnosis can induce a calm relaxed state of mind as can the use of Executive "Stress balls", a good walk in the open air and Aromatherapy help to avoid the "Meltdowns" caused by the sheer sensory impact and pressures of modern life.

Why do these things work?

The reason goes back to our look at the EEG machines which monitor the electrical activity in the brain through soft painless electrodes taped to the scalp. These reveal that the activity of the brain varies through five distinct frequencies or "brainwaves", the same as radio stations do. In the brain these frequencies are Delta, Theta, Alpha, Beta and Gamma and each reflects the degree of excitation or relaxation of the brain and is a different shape of wave from each of the others, (as shown in the graph in the "Illustrations" section of this book) Delta are the longest, slowest waves with a beat of around 0.1-3.9 Hertz (Hz) and indicate a deep state of sleep, Theta waves, 4-7.9 Hz are associated with the less deep periods of the normal 90 minute sleep-cycle as well as with states of deep meditation and hypnosis. Alpha waves, 8-13.9 Hz are when you're calm, relaxed and attentive, perhaps watching TV, Beta waves 14-25 Hz dominate when thinking, working, very aware, active or worried. Gamma waves 25-100Hz signify complex intellectual tasks, Chess, advanced mathematics or extreme situations and/or pressure above 40Hz.

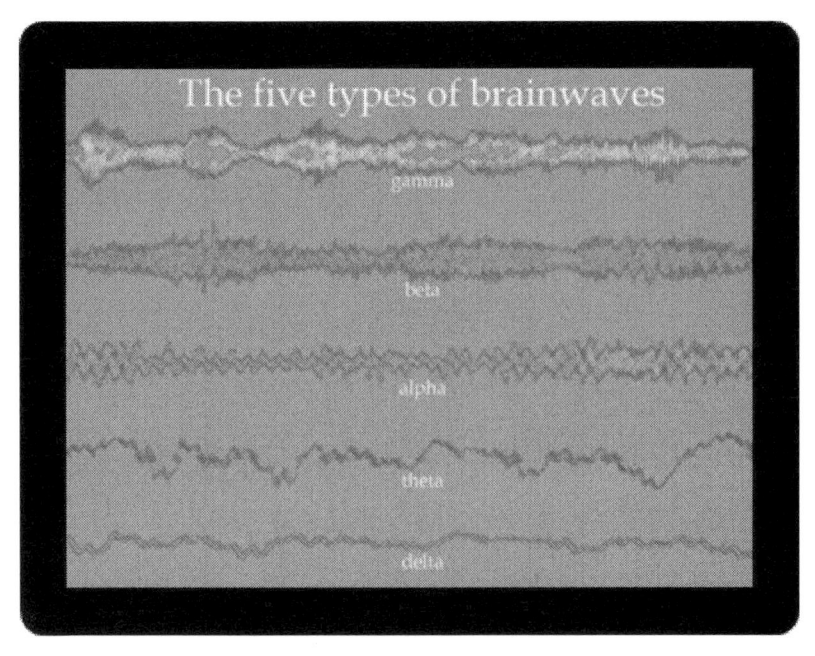

The five types of brainwaves

The types of activities described above like art therapy help to calm the brain down from over-stimulation toward the more relaxed states where healing takes place. The brain's patterns are in reality more complex than set out here and each frequency has its good and proper function, but if through stress, particularly with Autistic imbalance towards the more active frequencies continues for too long, "Meltdowns" or "Freak-outs" will result as the brain produces too much "noise" from too many contradictory rapid signals. HFAs, if not all Autists derive their creativity, hyper-ness, sleep problems and possibly a proportion of their gut problems from all this activity. Excess stress makes the body release a chemical called Cortisol made in the adrenal glands, sitting on top of each kidney. Cortisol makes us hyper and "ready-for-action" along with Adrenaline in threatening situations and usually returns safely to normal levels as soon as the danger has passed. However if the exposure is prolonged without a break-"de-stressing"- it causes immunological damage leaving some people (but not all) more prone to diseases like cancer or colds and damages the stomach and gut linings. Calming things helps re-adjust the balance and contributes towards achieving a stable, healthy and happy state of body and mind.

Please encourage your Autist to learn a sign language, whether British or American Sign Language (B/ASl). Both are internationally recognized non-verbal languages in their own right and learning grants are widely available. Some autistics/AS are poor verbal as well as non-verbal communicators and empowering them with another, essentially physical language will enhance their personal and social development well beyond anyone's expectations.

There are those who can be poor listeners or in the case of Dyslexics, readers/writers. Learning by eye and touch rather than ear can prove far more effective than standard classroom methods, even better it increases potential social opportunities to include that other special group of people who have to sign and as a bonus it can provide an immensely rewarding and lucrative career for those who are equipped to deal with either the mainstream or sheltered employment environment. Regarding adult employment conditions; employers may need to make provision for Autist/AS/Savant workers like quiet office space, lower light levels and if on a production line extra ear and tinted eye defenders. Gauze or other breathing masks reduce the chances of airborne irritants-dust, insects and pollen for outdoor workers and other contaminants for indoor ones. Gloves or suits/overalls do the same job protecting the skin from harmful chemicals and other reactive materials, basically just small tweaks to normal health and safety codes in the workplace.

On the subject of employment- it is hard for Aspies and especially gifted ones to hold down steady, long term employment. Repetitive or unstimulating tasks quickly get boring and stressful at times, leading to confrontation or a sudden resignation surprising everyone. Aspies "hold in" their feelings causing a buildup of tension until an apparently trivial incident ignites a strong reaction-one often misinterpreted as an overreaction. Aspies may not only frequently change jobs but also make several radical career changes during their working lives, looking for that elusive "right fit". In the current hostile economic times that can quickly lead to periods of severe financial hardship and the personal despair which can accompany them. It is important for Aspies to have sound financial planning and advice especially in the fields of savings, pensions and insurance inculcated into them in order to insulate them against their natural restless, creative and sometimes unwittingly destructive life pattern. Ideally that process should begin in the home as early as possible.

Sleep:

"For good health, make sleep a priority" wrote Lois E. Krahn, M.D. of the world famous Mayo Clinic, she is right for Autists, NTs, the young and the old. Lack of sleep contributes to lowered immunity, impaired performance at work, relationship breakdowns, brain cell death, which can lead to full-blown Autism, psychosis, premature aging and not least Alzheimer's, as described in The New Scientist journal, September 24th, 2009. It aids the formation of the deadly plaques we have discussed; use of sleep drugs reduces that formation. While not suggesting sleeping pills- usually either hypnotics or sedatives- as a first resort, if other things fail-use them and for as long as needed-under proper medical supervision. Do whatever it takes to get enough sleep at any age. Sleep is every bit as essential to a good life as food or water; for growth, maintenance, regeneration and happiness of body and mind. That is equally true with regards to seniors' health; it is also a total myth that people need less sleep as they get older (Fred Cicetti, Live Science, 10 May 2009) lack of sleep kills.

The minimum amount of sleep needed, except in very rare individuals like the late UK Prime Minister Margaret Thatcher for an adult is 6 hours a night; for optimum wellbeing the target is 8-9 hours and for children and adolescents, a lot more. Today we average three hours sleep less per night than our nineteenth Century Ancestors-and are seeing more mental illnesses than ever/ Even slight sleep deprivation causes tiredness (Lethargy), inability to learn and/or concentrate, unsafe driving and bad temper, how many children with AD(H)D or other such diagnoses are simply the victims of an ignorant home situation, kept up or out to all hours by selfish parents or ones who do not care about their children's outside or Online activities? Make no mistake at all: such parental/responsible adult behavior is a form of child abuse and teachers should react accordingly. How many totally normal children (or adults) are, along with their families the victims of social deprivation and whose parents or partners are blameless due to impossible circumstances?

Because of the unusual brain structure and CNS activity, good regular sleep, especially during the rigid times demanded by modern industrialized nations- the night- is hard for Autist/AS people, made worse by the extra sensitivity to sound, light, textures, allergies and so on. On the positive side that tendency gives some Autists the advantage of preferring working the better-paying night shifts with comfort and efficiency, benefitting both them and the employer. This perhaps relates to the Neanderthal Theory, Autists simply, in a sense cannot belong comfortably in that environment and need a simpler, older more natural lifestyle to thrive?

    An Autist child may sleep poorly or wake easily because of noises that their parents/caregivers can't hear, listen carefully to the child and act on what you are told. Sleep-deprivation explains many of the negatives experienced by both autistics and their carers. Actively involve the child in the construction of a good sleep environment and routine, explaining in detail what is being done and why, Aspies in particular ask a lot of questions as parents and teachers may already know☺. In a constantly noisy neighborhood white or pink noise machines work well. Non-toxic wadding, wood and old newspapers, wax or Silicone earplugs along with rubber wedges to dampen vibration provide a good alternative to expensive specialist soundproofing materials, as do aircraft-style "sleep kits" of muffles and eye masks to cut out both sound and light, heavy, dark drapes serve the same purpose Trust me, I've tried 'em all. The goal is to create a reassuring and reliable "sleep capsule" at a constant temperature of 70F for optimal effect and you have something which can benefit everyone of any age, NT or not for years. The earplugs are reusable and should be washed every day, Silicone ones also give the advantage of gently easing out earwax.

    Under medical supervision consider the use of the hormone Melatonin. These options will relax the child and by reducing anxiety in the short, medium and long term promote closer bonding from the extra trust created by success, bringing the child and the family, including brothers and sisters closer together. Love, reassurance, expressing confidence, support, and tolerance are all essentials. Parents and caregivers must though avoid excessive spoiling and over-protection – both perfectly natural reactions- but they can hinder healthy development and can "infantilize" a child throughout its whole life, to the point that it can never attain its full adult potential, exactly as many forms of abuse will. Overpraise too for no or trivial performance is equally bad, stunting the child's development and creating a Narcissistic personality which will be a heavy and isolating burden in later life. We all wish, for our children at least, that the world is made of candy floss-but it isn't and it does no-one any favors to pretend otherwise. That "line" between, protecting, coddling, spoiling and abuse can be very narrow and very grey, it will be found only after a long time and by trial and error because it varies with both changing circumstances and the natural personalities of the people and family traditions involved.

It is hard to do, accept that; take a deep breath and smile, if only at the irony of it all. Smiling alone, even if you don't mean it causes Endorphins to be released and you'll feel better and less frustrated for a while, giving you the chance to relax and regroup. Parents; please don't ever feel guilty about taking some time out for yourselves every now and then-you're human. You deserve it, you need it and it'll help you in all sorts of subtle ways in the years ahead. Guilt and resentment born of frustration can lead to anger and that is corrosive to any relationship.

Diet:

It's imperative for everyone to always remember that Autism is not any kind of disease, it can't be caught person to person, it can be helped and any advantages maximized, but there is no "cure", whatever claims may be made. There are also, as we've noted many branches to the Autism Family Tree as well as the Co-morbidities. Two very common ones are Crohn's and Celiac Disease, as well as other digressive irregularities. There are no completely verified global studies at this time of writing to prove it, but the recorded incidences by parents, Autists, Doctors, Specialists and teachers leave little question of their place in the family. Both are serious predominantly inherited illnesses, which affect men and women about equally, but smokers have more than double the risk of Crohn's than non-smokers. Both are autoimmune in origin and attack the whole gastrointestinal tract causing over time severe damage, pain, Rheumatoid arthritis, IBS, inflammation, nausea, rashes, eye problems and the loss of the body's ability to absorb vital nutrients and vitamins from food, resulting in bone loss, poor growth in children, depression, anemia and a host of other things. In severe untreated cases either condition can cause cancer or ulcers which can eat through the gut and without emergency surgery to remove and repair the damaged portion allow its contents to seep out into the trunk of the body, leading to probable blood-poisoning (Septicemia) and sometimes, death.

Both diseases initially target the small intestine and in neither instance do doctors really understand their causes, but they differ in other ways. Celiac tends to present earlier in life, making diagnosis easier. Celiac patients don't normally run a fever and the two conditions although they have a great deal in common including Autism; have different triggers. Celiac is triggered predominantly by the protein gluten, found in numerous things; bread, pasta, wheat, barley, semolina, fried things, butter, cakes, soups, beer and a whole lot more. The top treatment for Celiac is a gluten-free diet, but it doesn't always work without help. Other treatments are fairly common for both diseases, anti-inflammatory medications, steroids, painkillers and Immune system suppressing drugs to diminish the severity of the body's reaction to whatever it is intolerant to, gluten in Celiac, Crohn's, we don't know. Neither is curable, but they are, with careful lifestyle choices and specialist monitoring, usually manageable throughout life. Diagnosis is through blood and/or allergy testing, scans and perhaps a gut biopsy in difficult cases. Whatever the result reducing the possible allergens reduces the impact of the disease. I counsel patients to have the full blood tests for allergies; airborne, waterborne, insect, plant, fungi and food and to undergo the "Scratch-test", where shallow scratches are made on the skin, usually on the back or upper arm and a suspected allergen is brushed on. If the skin erupts, -it's another irritant to avoid- if not, it's OK. Pin and patch testing follow the same principle.

To save money, with great care and after medical instruction you can do your own scratch test at home. Disinfect your skin and get a small blunt needle. Dip it in a suspected allergen, like bran and just graze, but don't puncture the skin, wait 10 minutes to see if a red welt comes up, indicating a reaction. This isn't too accurate, has some risk (infection and anaphylaxis) and the needle should be disinfected with boiling water after each test, but where a lack of facilities or money exists, it's better than nothing-I have experimented with it on myself a number of times successfully.

Milk:

Cow's milk is a very common cause of irritation and intolerance. Firstly, at least 60% of adults cannot digest it and the figure is higher among the Asian community (USA Today, August 30th, 2009). It contains Lactose, an acidic sugar to which many people, myself included have a sharp intolerance, milk is also high in Gluten, causing the problem with cakes, butter etc. for Celiac patients and fourthly virtually all animal milk has Casein in it, a Phosphoprotein which is used in paint-making-as well as ice-cream, pastries and other foodstuffs. Again, intolerance levels are high and can be severe...and there is some, as yet inconclusive evidence tying its consumption to Autism.

The Elimination Method:

This is an approach to reducing irritants which offers many advantages and a couple of disadvantages: It is free, thorough and accurate and if done carefully, riskless. The disadvantages; it's very painstaking and time-consuming. Basically you note every single thing you eat, drink or are otherwise exposed to-including household substances such as laundry liquid- over a month and then eliminate one at a time. This means NO exposure at all to it for 2-4 weeks. If you feel better, note the substance and avoid it, if not, it's safe for you. Then move on to the next one until the list of dos and donts is completed. This works, but can take 6-12 months to complete; many people find that well worth it, because diet affects mood and consciousness and by eliminating irritants Autistic conditions such as ADD/ADHD to name but two have been improved greatly and in some people almost completely cured. On top of that, anything which helps improve physical health, improves mental and emotional health as well. "Mind follows body-every time" (Hale).

Conclusion:

A main reason for writing this book was to answer some questions and provide some background and context on the subject, which leaves one important question unanswered. American President John F Kennedy said, "What makes journalism so fascinating and biography so interesting is the struggle to answer that single question, 'What's he like'?" (Ben Bradlee, Conversations with Kennedy). That is the question I shall now try to answer about Autism from my Aspie perspective, "what's it like"?

"Well…it's very like living in a greenhouse; the greater the extent of the Autism, the thicker and darker is the glass and the tighter the windows and door are sealed. You can see and hear us, as we can you, but most of the time it is slightly distorted, sometimes physically, always emotionally and "out of synch", like watching a movie at the wrong speed or hearing a language you know but in an unknown grammar or accent, you understand-and you don't fully understand at the same time- there's void somewhere, it's hard. It is by turns a frustrating, sometimes frightening and frequently confusing situation for everyone. At other times being inside that greenhouse is an extraordinarily sublime and heightened experience of thought without distraction in which some, like Tesla and others found moments of profound clarity in which they uncovered higher knowledge of arts, sciences and nature that have radically altered and enhanced our view of the world around us, they were able to "escape the chains of the ordinary" (Hale). Take a step inside and see; the door is open.

Selected Reading and Resources:

Aarons, M and Gittens T (1992)   The Autistic Continuum:

An assessment and

Intervention schedule

Berkshire NFER Nelson

Attwood, T (1998)   Asperger's Syndrome.

London. Jessica Kingsley.

Badcock, CR (2009)   The Imprinted Brain:
Amazon Books

Baron-Cohen, S (2003)   The Essential Difference: Male and Female Brains and The Truth about Autism.
Cambridge. Basic Books.

Baron-Cohen, S (1992)   Debate and Argument on Modularity and Development in Autism: A reply to Burack.
Journal of Child Psychology and Psychiatry:
Volume 33, Number 3 pp. 623-629

Bruce, C (1998)   Freefall
Little, Brown and Company, New York

Ehlers, S and Gillberg, C (1993   The Epidemiology of Asperger's Syndrome

Journal of Child Psychology and Psychiatry

Fitzgerald, M   Autism and Creativity: Is There a Link between Autism in Men and Exceptional Ability? November 2003, Routledge) (In this author's opinion, "yes")

Fitzgerald, M The Genesis of Artistic Creativity: Asperger's Syndrome and the Arts - July 2005.

Jessica Kingsley Publisher London

Gardner, H (1983)   Frames of Mind: The Theory of Multiple Intelligence

New York, Basic Books

Grandin, T (2008)   The Way I see it

New York Barnes and Noble

ICD-10, (1992)   World Health Organization

Geneva. WHO Press

Kendall, P (2001) Childhood Disorders

Philadelphia: Temple University Press.

Kottek, C (1994) 6th Edition: Anthropology: The Exploration of Human Diversity

New York: McGraw Hill.

Kraepelin, E (1927) 9th Edition: Textbook of Psychiatry.

Munich. University Press

Powell, S, and Jordan R (Ed) (2000): Autism and Learning (A guide to Good Practice).

London, David Fulton Publications

Prakash, V. (2001)   A Short Note On The Theory Of Multiple Intelligence

    Mysore University

Reiss, AL and Dant CC (2003)   the behavioral neurogenetics of Fragile X Syndrome analyzing gender brain behavior Relationships in child Developmental Psychopathologies: Volume 15 pp. 927- 952

Remme, W et al (2005)   Study of Heart failure Awareness and Per (SHAPE)

    European Heart Journal

    September 2005.

Ridley, M (2000)   Genome.

    New York. Harper Perennial

Rostick, E (2006)   Male and Female Hormone Testing

    Life Extension Magazine:

    Volume 12 Number 11:

Sanger Institute, (2001)   The Human Genome Project.

                                            Cambridge. Sanger Institute Publications

Schnable, P (2008).   Iowa State University.

                                              Archives of The Center for Plant Genomics.

Sulston, J (2002)   The Common Thread.

                                              London, Corgi Books

Various, (2007)   Diagnostic and Statistical Manual of Mental Disorders (DSM IV)

                                              American Psychiatric Association, Arlington, Virginia

Various, (2003)   Journal of the Autism Society of America (ASA)

Bethesda, Maryland.

Venkatesan, S, (2004)　　　Children with Developmental Disabilities
New Delhi, Sage Publications

Volkmar, F Chawarska, K and Klin, I (2005)) Autism in Infancy and Early Childhood
Annual Review of Psychology Volume 56, pp. 315-336.

Wall, K (2004)　　　Autism and Early Years Practice.
London, Paul Chapman Publications

Wilson, R (2003)　　　Special Education Needs in the Early Years.
London, Routledge-Falmer

Wood, D (1998) 2nd Edition How Children think and learn
Oxford, Blackwell Publishing.

World Health Organization: (2006)   WHO Archives

Wurtzel, E (1995)   Prozac Nation.

New York. Riverhead Books

Zulkardi, N (1999)   CASCADE-MEI Thesis

Enschede: University of Twente Publication.

Seminar and Conference minutes:

Spiker, D (1999):   Seminar. April 1999.

Department of Psychiatry and Behavioral Sciences

Stanford University, School of Medicine

Walton, J (1999)   Seminar June 2nd

The art and science of teaching music/dance

Stanford University, Department of Education

Whiteley, P (2004). The Durham Conference Proceedings Durham University (UK).

Journals:

Annals of Dyslexia;

Dutch home-based pre-reading intervention with children at familial risk of dyslexia: Sandra G. van Otterloo, Aryan van der Leij. December 2009, Volume 59, Issue 2, pp. 169-195

Io9

The Lancet

Mensa Monthly

Nature Genetics, (2007)   February 21, Issue

Nature Genetics, (2007)   March 17, Issue

New Scientist

Psychiatry, jwatch.org   December 10th, 2012 Steven Dubovsky, MD

A predictor for PTSD In deployed soldiers, high pre-deployment CO_2 reactivity was associated with risk for developing PTSD

Scientific American

Science 2.0

Wired Magazine

Credits and grateful thanks to:

Prof David P Burkart: Alembic Enterprises (University of Miami): For Artworks, proof-reading and belief.

Mr. John Goodfellow: BSc: Editor.

Ms Peggy A. Leyva: Support and professional critique.

Mr. Alan Murdoch (University of Birmingham): Technical consultation.

Mr. William Wallace: Whose idea this book was and whose advice was invaluable.

Mr. Stu Watson. All Cover Art and Resolution: Contact: stuartwatson4888@gmail.com

Additional graphic Images: "Couchtripper".

Disclaimer:

By reading this book you confirm and agree to the statements and Disclaimer set forth herein.

The content represents only itself and the information at the date of publication. As conditions or knowledge change, The Author fully reserves the right to alter and/or update it to reflect those new conditions, but is under no obligation at any time to either alter or update the contents of this book. This book is firstly a personal and secondly a professional narrative of knowledge and experience. The Author does not assume any responsibility for errors, inaccuracies or omissions in any of the statements, articles or information in this book. Any products, resources and information (individually and collectively referred to in this book are for information and reference purposes only and are not intended as a replacement or substitute for the advice of a qualified doctor or specialist. Any reliance upon the material in this book is at the Reader's discretion.

Printed in Great Britain
by Amazon